RELIGIOUS
CONFUSION

LAWRENCE NEISENT

RELIGIOUS CONFUSION

FINDING CLARITY AND CONFIDENCE IN GOD'S PURPOSE FOR YOUR LIFE

TATE PUBLISHING
AND ENTERPRISES, LLC

Scripture quotations marked (MSG) are taken from *The Message*. Copyright © 1993, 1994, 1995, 1996, 2000, 2001, 2002. Used by permission of NavPress Publishing Group.

Scripture quoted by permission. Quotations designated (NET) are from the NET Bible® copyright ©1996-2006 by Biblical Studies Press, L.L.C. http://bible.org All rights reserved. This material is available in its entirety as a free download or online web use at http://netbible.org/.

Scripture quotations marked (NIV) are taken from the *Holy Bible, New International Version*®, NIV®. Copyright © 1973, 1978, 1984 by Biblica, Inc.™ Used by permission of Zondervan. All rights reserved worldwide. www.zondervan.com

Scripture quotations marked (NKJV) are taken from the *New King James Version*. Copyright © 1982 by Thomas Nelson, Inc. Used by permission. All rights reserved.

Scripture quotations marked (NLT) are taken from the *Holy Bible, New Living Translation*, copyright © 1996. Used by permission of Tyndale House Publishers, Inc., Wheaton, Illinois 60189. All rights reserved.

Scripture quotations marked (TLB) are taken from *The Living Bible* / Kenneth N. Taylor: Tyndale House, © Copyright 1997, 1971 by Tyndale House Publishers, Inc. Used by permission. All rights reserved.

This book is designed to provide accurate and authoritative information with regard to the subject matter covered. This information is given with the understanding that neither the author nor Tate Publishing, LLC is engaged in rendering legal, professional advice. Since the details of your situation are fact dependent, you should additionally seek the services of a competent professional.

The opinions expressed by the author are not necessarily those of Tate Publishing, LLC.

Published by Tate Publishing & Enterprises, LLC
127 E. Trade Center Terrace | Mustang, Oklahoma 73064 USA
1.888.361.9473 | www.tatepublishing.com

Tate Publishing is committed to excellence in the publishing industry. The company reflects the philosophy established by the founders, based on Psalm 68:11,

"The Lord gave the word and great was the company of those who published it."

Book design copyright © 2016 by Tate Publishing, LLC. All rights reserved.
Cover design by Lirey Blanco
Interior design by Manolito Bastasa

Published in the United States of America

ISBN: 978-1-68352-101-3
1. Religion / Christian Life / Personal Growth
2. Religion / Christian Life / Spiritual Growth
16.08.19

Contents

Foreword

THIS BOOK SHOULD come with a warning label! In a society that says it's all about stability and happiness, we see imbalance, dissatisfaction (no matter how successful or famous they become), and self-doubt polluting the lives of people God is so in love with.

Religious Confusion brings holy perspective and returns the bar to its original place by making Jesus our measuring stick, challenging our Christianity to carry the same fruit as He did. I appreciate the transparency of a seasoned leader who doesn't just share his highlights, but teaches firsthand revelation from challenges and obstacles he has had to face to deliver this timely word with great accuracy.

This book will be an answer to prayer to so many looking for clarity on what it means to live as a believer in this modern era. As a leader whose focus is training the next generation of influencers, I've longed for a clear message to be proclaimed on what it is to be a Christian both in the spotlight and behind the scenes. I've watched as this current generation is busy chasing fads of Christianity and polarities of opinion and doctrine instead of focusing on *who* matters most—Jesus—and letting Him have all of them!

Religious Confusion is a turning point for those who've been in the church for decades and a foundational resource for those who have just recently committed their lives to Jesus. No matter where you are, get ready to have your priorities reset, your heart fine-tuned, and your confusion turn to clarity as you read through the pages of this timely message.

—Chris Estrada
Director of Youth Ministries at Christ
for the Nations Institute
Founder of Chris Estrada Ministries

Introduction

"NEVER IN THE history of the world has any society so successfully caused the church to deviate from scripture."

It was like a numbing explosion went off as my wife, Tracy, spoke these words. This conversation triggered the most painful and purposeful season I had ever known as a church leader, but even more so, as a Christian. What have we become? More importantly, what must we do to become more like Jesus?

Jesus loves the church. If our goal is to be more like Jesus, then we must choose to love the church. Instead of choosing to love the church, some people have chosen to leave the church. In all fairness, we must acknowledge that in some cases, it's not because they are abandoning their faith, but because they are trying to preserve it. Rather than abandon-

> GOD IS NOT TRYING TO DRAW PEOPLE INTO OUR BELIEFS. GOD IS DRAWING PEOPLE INTO HIS LOVE.

ing the church, we must decide to rediscover her on our faith journey as we inspire and empower the next generation to rise up and be the church Jesus wants them to be!

Instead of telling people what we are against, we must show them what we are about. Imagine a world where the church becomes a true expression of Jesus Christ through loving, serving, and giving sacrificially.

> IF WE GET PEOPLE TO COME TO OUR CHURCHES BUT AREN'T EFFECTIVELY MAKING DISCIPLES, WE ARE ONLY CONTRIBUTING TO THE GREATER PROBLEM OF DISILLUSIONMENT IN OUR SOCIETY.

Largely the world has the wrong idea about the church because Christians have the wrong idea about themselves. Jesus didn't die so we could go to church.

Let's gather together as the church and be mobilized to be the church that is the Jesus movement of our generation! People ministering to people as a way of life is what will change the world.

Chapter 1

Results, Not Pursuits

DRIVING DOWN THE familiar street where my family used to live, I waved at our former neighbor who was standing in his yard. The next thing I remember was that neighbor pounding on my driver's side window unable to open my door because of the collision. Another car backed out of their driveway as I was looking away to wave. The impact was severe, slamming me into the rearview mirror, lacerating my face and knocking me unconscious for a few minutes. I spent several hours trying to be still as the doctor carefully removed tiny shards of glass from numerous cuts across my cheek and eyebrow. Finally, I was stitched up and ready to be taken home with half of my face bandaged, feeling and looking slightly mummified.

Robert was one of my good friends. He stopped by to check on me, asking if he could help in any way. He offered to get my things out of my car that was totaled and inquired where to find it. I told him where the car had been towed, thanking him for his offer but explaining it wasn't necessary as we intended to take care of this after I had taken a few days to recover. Robert knew I had recently purchased an expensive new car stereo. His compassionate efforts were actually efforts to steal my new system, which he did. It would be several years later before I would have a passing conversation with another "friend" who would mention to me what Robert had done. Robert would later have an affair with the wife of another one of his "friends."

The most dangerous enemy to our lives is the enemy we count as a friend. Inviting somebody whose motives aren't in our best interest into our lives leaves us vulnerable as we unknowingly empower their destructive efforts. The ability to determine what is helpful and what is hurtful is vital to our overall well-being. When you find yourself questioning what everybody around you seems to be embracing, it can be confusing. Robert seemed like such a great guy who wanted to help, and I was in such a state of need. Had I questioned his efforts, it could have caused others to think I was just being paranoid or irrational.

As we begin this journey together of exploring religious confusion, I need to expose one of your closest friends. I regret to inform you that this friend has likely gained full access to your life, and when I question him, it will likely be disturbing, and your first response may be more of a reaction. This friend is "the pursuit of happiness," and it seems everybody in our modern-day culture has invited him into the center of his or her lives. This idea is so central to our way of thinking that our first response is to defend and protect the very thing that consistently overpromises and underdelivers throughout all the years of our lives.

The pursuit of happiness appears to be a friend with our best interests in mind, but this pursuit is never satisfied. In addition, this way of thinking seeps into every area of our lives and emerges in every attitude we hold. Life becomes more about my pleasure than it is about God's purposes. The basis of religious confusion is allowing life to deviate from the ultimate goal of loving God and loving others. Don't misunderstand. God is delighted when we are fulfilled according to his wonderful purposes. However, our fulfillment according to any other standard is a counterfeit that results in an endlessly unfulfilling pursuit.

TRUE HAPPINESS IS A RESULT, NOT A PURSUIT.

God designed us to experience pleasure, but he never intended for us to make pleasure our priority in life. When happiness becomes your priority, it escapes you. We are designed to worship God, and God alone. Self-fulfillment as a focus becomes an expression of self-worship, robbing us of our joy. Interestingly, when I was perusing a bookstore, I noticed the number one self-help topic seemed to be ideas on how to be happy and successful. Then I realized the next most prevalent topic I observed was how to conquer depression. When we exchange the eternal purposes of God for the temporal pursuits of this world, disappointment and depression are inevitable.

> So do not worry, saying, "What shall we eat?" or "What shall we drink?" or "What shall we wear?" For the pagans run after all these things, and your heavenly Father knows that you need them. But seek first his kingdom and his righteousness, and all these things will be given to you as well. (Matt. 6:31–33, NIV)

When my daughters were six and seven years old, we had an astonishing experience in our front yard. My oldest daughter, Faith, was just standing there looking at me when a butterfly landed on her shoulder. She stood very still as I took a picture. My younger daughter, Lexi, was filled with anticipation to have her turn with a butterfly landing on her. She ran, jumped, grasped, and did all she could to coerce the butterfly in her direction but to no avail. I finally calmed her down and asked her to stand very still with her arms out to her side pretending to be a tree. Within just a few seconds, the butterfly landed on her as well.

We no longer live "in want" when we discover the joy of resting in the presence of God. This is the place where good things begin following us in life, and we stop grasping at the things we want God to give us. We don't follow them, but rather, they follow us because they are results, not pursuits. He is our loving shepherd who cares for our souls and fulfills our lives.

"The LORD is my shepherd, I shall not be in want… Surely goodness and love will follow me all the days of my life, and I will dwell in the house of the LORD forever" (Psalm 23:1, 6 KJV).

When we make results our pursuits, confusion abounds. The Bible compares marriage interaction of the husband and wife to the interaction of Jesus and the church. In our society, marriage has become one of the main tools we use in our pursuit of happiness. It's very common for single people to be in the pursuit of marrying somebody who will make them happy. There is a huge problem with this, however. If we are relying on somebody else for happiness, we aren't loving them—we are using them.

What if we have this all wrong? What if God's plan is not for marriage to be an avenue we pursue to make us happy? What if God's plan for marriage is that it's an avenue we pursue to become more like Jesus? This changes the primary purpose of marriage from happiness to holiness. A lot of modern-day theology seems to be based on some idea that God's primary concern is to empower us in our pursuit of happiness. Some churches have given weeks of emphasis to helping couples understand God's desire for married couples to have great sex. I'm not sure God's all that concerned with this, as much as He is concerned with our having healthy marriages born out of wonderful friendship with God and with each other. The result of a wonderful friendship producing a healthy marriage will be incredible intimacy on every level of life. Again, it seems this is reversing the order and making results into our pursuits.

It's true that God wants you to have the most incredible life you can possibly imagine. The confusion comes when we fail to realize that this amazing life doesn't come from pursuing it but rather providing it for others. It truly is more blessed to give than to receive. The pursuit of blessedness involves the pursuit of giving more than receiving. The pursuit of happiness is about me, while the pursuit of blessedness is about others. It's interesting that the pursuit of blessedness, which is about others, does more for me than the pursuit of happiness ever could. Making the most of our lives doesn't make other people's pain go away. But making other people's pain go away does make the most of our lives.

Nathan, Renee, and their four children are dear friends who have become family to our family. Their daughter, Aleah, has had to see specialists to address a physical condition she battles. In one instance, they had traveled to

Baltimore for a week of treatment. The temperature outside was cold, and the entire situation was inconvenient and uncomfortable. Aleah, aged eight at the time, was frustrated by the trip, procedures, weather, etc. On their way to their appointment, she was voicing her frustration for having to be doing what they were doing. Something happened that day that completely changed her perspective. During her treatment, she met another little girl who had been in an accident where a swing set had fallen over, landing on the back of her neck, paralyzing her from the neck down.

Aleah befriended the little girl and began serving her and trying to make her experience as pleasant as possible. Suddenly, the inconvenience of her trip, the weather, and her uncomfortable procedures lost their grip on her attitude. Trying to ease the other little girl's suffering that was greater than Aleah's seemed to rescue her from her own frustrations. It was very impacting when they returned and her daddy, Nathan, shared this story. His

> GOD'S GREATEST PRIORITY ISN'T FOR US TO LEARN THE HAPPINESS OF LIVING LIFE SO WONDERFULLY. GOD'S HEART IS FOR US TO DISCOVER THE JOY OF GIVING LIFE SO FREELY.

words continue to remain in my heart to this day. "Jesus delivers us from our sin. Our willingness to participate in other people's suffering delivers us from ourselves."

We've raised up a generation of Christians who have a complete aversion to anything inconvenient. We've all been trained that God's foremost concern is our happiness. The problem is that happiness is the world's substitute for joy! It's this pursuit of happiness that is flawed right up front with selfishness that keeps us from getting any area of life right.

This is what we see in the loving, serving, giving example of Jesus Christ. Jesus wasn't born for his pleasure. Jesus was born for God's purpose. You and I were not born for our pleasure. We were born for God's purposes.

Questions to Consider for a Discussion Among Friends or Perhaps in a Small Group

ATHLETES RUNNING ALONE DON'T SET WORLD RECORDS.

Consider the relationships God has entrusted to your care and invite someone to go deeper with you. Not only will it help you, but it could deeply impact a person's life by simply inviting them to join you on your journey. You don't have to have things all figured out to invite others to grow with you in the process of becoming more like Jesus.

Doing this positions you to provide something for others rather than merely receiving something for yourself. To *inspire* literally means to "breathe into." Beware of a life that is merely inspired and never empowered. We must not only be inspired (inhale), but we must also learn to be empowered (exhale), purposing to inspire other people.

The ideas expressed in this book are not surface ideas to merely be read and appreciated. These concepts address an overall paradigm that must be challenged. The ideas must be digested through conversation and interaction to truly run their course and have an impact. Again, athletes running alone don't set world records. Who you can you invite to run with you on this journey?

Understanding why we are so given to selfish pursuits requires us to look beyond the surface issues in life.

Discussion Questions

1. What are some of the ways you have pursued happiness for your life?
2. What about your life speaks of God's purpose more than your pleasure? What about your life speaks of your pleasure more than God's purpose?

3. What are some things that try to keep you from resting in God's presence, and what can you do to conquer those things?

4. When you think about a person whose life is an expression of God's purposes, who do you think of, and why?

5. When you think about what you currently do to bless others, what comes to mind? What is something you can begin to do in order to more intentionally bless the lives of other people?

Scripture References for Further Reading and Study

Matthew 6:31–33 (NIV)
Psalm 23:1–6 (KJV)

Deep Beneath the Obvious

FAITH AND LEXI were three and two years old respectively. Both girls were enamored with the latest stuffed animal that had been added to our family, Nemo. This wasn't your usual, small stuffed animal. This was bigger than life-size at almost three-feet long! The girls had their own beds, but they shared a room, and each night, they took turns having Nemo sleep with them. One night, a very compassionate older sister shouted with great concern to her parents. It was Lexi's turn to have Nemo in her bed for the night, and with great concern, we heard Faith shouting, "Mom, Dad! Hurry! Come put Nemo in my bed. Lexi has him, and I'm afraid she might choke on him!"

I'm not sure how long she'd been lying there formulating this battle plan. Somewhere along the way, she picked up on our concern that the girls could choke on small toys. My wife, Tracy, and I could not contain our laughter as the presented concern was that her younger sister might choke on this toy that was about the same size as her sister.

At a very young age, we learn to cooperate with hidden agendas and masked master plans. Many times we aren't even aware we are doing this as we are simply embracing some deeper pursuit that could very easily been born from some dysfunction in our past. Everybody in fallen humanity possesses certain dysfunctions, whether we realize it or not. We are all more driven by dysfunction than any of us care to admit.

Deep beneath the obvious bruised emotions and scarred souls produce reactions of great magnitude. If my mom gets anywhere near a bird, her heart begins to race, and she becomes keenly aware of where she is in proximity to the bird, no matter how small it may be. This all stems back to when she was a child and a blue jay, known to be an aggressive bird, attacked her and scratched her face for getting too close to its nest. That one incident from her childhood affected her awareness of all birds for the rest of her life.

My household culture was very intense when I was growing up. My dad's common phrase to us was, "Hurry up!" We were all loud and aggressive in our approach to communication. My sister and I were very aggressive about our conflicts and arguments, even at times getting physical to get our way over something as simple as what to watch on television. There is a certain level of intensity I possess as a result of growing up in this atmosphere and experiencing a pressurized approach to life as a child.

My intensity is one of my greatest strengths. My intensity is one of my greatest weaknesses as well. I'm capable of provoking a lot of forward-thinking progress, planning, and strategic implementation to get somewhere. Many times I find myself saying to our team, "Hurry up!" I don't say it in so few words as I have learned to mask my dysfunction as a concern that nobody chokes on a three-foot-long Nemo!

Many driven leaders are secretly motivated by the fear of failure, the desire to please people, or the pursuit of recognition. What in your life quietly and consistently emerges from your heart? Your heart is the source of everything you do. The Bible describes the heart as the wellspring of life. This means your heart is the source of everything else in your life. Your heart overflows into thoughts, words, and actions.

"Above all else, guard your heart, for it is the wellspring of life" (Proverbs 4:23, NIV).

Roots in our lives are found in the heart. These roots are the source of what we believe and determine how we behave. God is constantly trying to reach beyond our behavior to get to our hearts. Religion can only reach our behavioral conclusions. It's a relationship with Jesus from our hearts that begin to affect the root structure behind all behavior.

Jacob wrestled with God in pursuit of God's blessing. The blessing of God isn't about something that is given to you but something that is awakened in you. God's response to Jacob's pursuit was transformation: "I will not let you go unless you bless me." The man asked him, "What is your name?" "Jacob," he answered. Then the man said, "Your name will no longer be Jacob, but Israel…" (Genesis 32:26–28, NIV).

This name change was significant. Even in our culture, we understand that covenant relationship commonly produces a name change. My wife took my last name the day we stood at the altar devoting our lives together in marriage. The name *Jacob* means deceiver. Of course, Jacob deceived his father to steal his brother's blessing. This changing of Jacob's name at the time when he was pursuing the blessing of God speaks of transformation. Jacob was in the process of becoming Israel. Bible commentators differ on the literal meaning of the name *Israel*, but consistently, the name communicates the idea of prevailing, rulership, and authority.

It's interesting to note that this name change speaks of moving from carnal deception to victorious living. With this in mind, we see something in Isaiah 27 that we might miss otherwise.

"In days to come, Jacob will take root, Israel will bud and blossom and fill all the world with fruit" (Isaiah 27:6, NIV).

Notice that it's the natural man that must be dealt with in hidden and secret places deep beneath the obvious, where roots are discovered. Then after growth occurs in the roots, the spiritual man begins to blossom and sprout, producing fruit. The key to bearing much fruit is having healthy roots! Outside of Christ, we get rooted in confusion and frustration.

> THE STRUGGLE FOR A TREE IS NEVER PRODUCING FRUIT IN THE SKY BUT RATHER FINDING NUTRIENTS IN THE DIRT.

The heart is more powerful and influential than any of us realize. The next time you find yourself waiting for a long train to pass, start counting how many cars are in the train. As you do consider that your heart pumps enough blood in your lifetime to fill two hundred of the tankers in the lineup. This is 1.5 million barrels![1] Your heart beats about one hundred thousand times every day![2] This means your

---

[1] "15 Facts About Your Heart That Are Hard To Believe," accessed June 24, 2016, http://www.top.me/fitness/15-facts-about-your-own-heart-that-are-hard-to-believe-7897.html.

[2] *The Wellness Beat*, Volume 3, Issue 4, February 2015, accessed June 24, 2016, http://www.nonotuck.com/wp-content/uploads/2015/02/Wellness-Newsletter-12.pdf.

heart will beat more than thirty-six million times in the next year of your life! By the time you are seventy years old, your heart will have beaten 2.5 billion times!

The physical mission of the heart is astonishing! The emotional mission of the heart is equally as fascinating. When my daughters receive an award at school for academic accomplishment or good behavior, there is something so powerful in my heart that beams with energy! On the contrary, when somebody cuts me off in traffic or takes "my parking space," there's something very powerful in my heart that drives me to irrational anger. Emotions are so powerful that the heart is capable of completely sabotaging our lives if left unchecked.

Our motives are seated deep beneath the obvious behaviors of our lives and aren't always easily identified. Tracy began noticing that I was getting up to work earlier and earlier. My justification was how wonderful God's presence was in my times of prayer at sacrificial times of the morning. In addition, it was amazing how productive I was before the rest of the world was awake and communicating with me. Finally, when my alarm invaded the 3:00 a.m. atmosphere of our bedroom, we had a "discussion."

My explanation unveiled extreme viewpoints that needed her wisdom as I rationalized of our limited number of years and the fleeting time we have to discover why we were put on this planet. My most irrational conclusion finally came at the end of my impressive speech, "Sleep is a waste of time!" In that moment, I realized something was motivating me more than noble efforts to leave the world a better place. We implemented the 4:00 a.m. rule: no alarms before 4:00 a.m.

The pursuit of success is something that people readily applaud in our society. If we aren't careful, our pursuit begins to be shaped by a thirst for applause. Successful leaders are many times celebrated while being driven by unhealthy motives that exist deep beneath the obvious. The fear of failure, a desire for recognition, or a host of other unhealthy driving forces can produce outrageous behaviors, pursuits, and expectations in a person. Driven leaders take their toll on people while inspiring leaders leave their mark on people.

So much of what we've done in the name of God in the church over the generations has been born from human dysfunction rather than the loving, serving, giving heart of Jesus. Religious reactions produced from confused motives and deep-seated dysfunction easily make way for religious confusion. Only God can help us discover these deeply recessed areas of our heart. David cries out for God's help with his heart in a way that is very insightful: "Search me, O God, and know my heart; test me and know my anxious thoughts. See if there is any offensive way in me, and lead me in the way everlasting" (Psalm 139:23–24, NIV).

One day while reading this, I realized that David had said something very interesting at the beginning of this chapter that almost negates what he's saying at the end: "O LORD, you have searched me and you know me...before a word is on my tongue you know it completely" (Psalm 139:1, 4 NIV)

AS CHRISTIANS, WE BELIEVE WHAT WE BELIEVE, BUT WE LOVE WHAT WE LOVE EVEN MORE THAN WE BELIEVE WHAT WE BELIEVE. THIS IS WHY GOD IS ALWAYS DEALING WITH OUR HEARTS!

If God has already searched him and knows him so completely that before a word is spoken God is aware that it's coming, then why does David ask him to search his heart? David wasn't asking God to search his heart for God to know David. David was asking God to search his heart so David could know David.

Character defects grow for years beneath the surface of our lives. We prefer to project the image of adequacy rather than taking an honest and unsettling look at ourselves. Even if we present our best smile, it doesn't work out that well if we have something in our teeth. Only a true friend will tell you when something's just not right. Truly, it is not good for man to be alone.

Discussion Questions

Remember, athletes running alone don't set world records. Take someone with you.

1. What are some common behaviors of people who are secretly motivated by fear of failure? (The desire to please people, pursuit of recognition, etc.)
2. What actions do you have in place to guard your heart? What else can you do to more effectively expose and address the deeper motives of your life?
3. What does it mean to you to "have healthy roots"? How have you established healthy roots, and how is this helping you bear good fruit?
4. When you think of a person whose pursuit of happiness is shaped by the applause of others, what does that look like?
5. Spend some time asking God to search your heart. Purpose to talk to someone you trust about what God reveals to you. Who is that person?

Scripture References for Further Reading and Study

Proverbs 4:23 (NIV)
Genesis 32:26–28 (NIV)
Isaiah 27:6 (NIV)
Psalm 139 (NIV)

Chapter 3

Community

"HI! HOW ARE you?"

"Fine! How are you?"

"Doing well. How is the church?"

"Church is great! How about your church?"

"Things are good. God bless you. Have a great day."

"You too!"

This was my conversation with a pastor from our area who is a fellow member of a local service organization. Week after week, we would see each other at this meeting where many of us from the community gathered to join efforts and make our world a better place. Everything was fine until one day the conversation deviated from the disingenuous routine of conversational rhetoric.

In the middle of our surface pleasantries, something happened that day that changed my life. We actually went deeper into a place where most conversations never dare to go. It's that place where communication actually leads to vulnerable connection between two people. This is the place called community, and it's very enriching!

Most relationships never achieve this status because it's risky business to actually connect on this level. This level of connection requires something of a sacrifice. For a few years, this pastor and I had seemingly stood on two sides of the altar of friendship exchanging surface expressions and casual communication without ever really offering anything sacrificial. But this day, it all changed. Suddenly, the casual conversation over the altar shifted as my friend bypassed the chitchat and flung himself upon the altar, risking everything to tell me of a personal struggle. This pastor told me about his sin.

"Hi! How are you?" He initiated with hand extended as had happened countless times before. "Great! How are you?" I responded, receiving the handshake in sync and in rhythm, now awaiting the volley back to my side of the court. Then it happened. The grip tightened, and a mere handshake was transformed into an intentional embrace. He pulled me slightly toward himself as if he was inviting me to move beyond that usual personal space of about two feet. Taken by surprise at the completely different rhythm of our conversation, I found myself leaning in with uncertainty, not really sure what was taking place. That's when he said those words that transformed our casual connection into a meaningful relationship. Everything about our friendship changed that day when he simply said, "I'm not doing very well. Can we talk?"

Within sixty seconds, our relationship that had existed for several years went to a relational level that neither of us expected. Two months prior, I had been asked to be a speaker in our public forum meeting. I had shared a message of hope and help through Jesus Christ explaining my life story, which included a past of drug involvement. This man had been waiting for the right moment to invite me into his struggle with an addiction as a result. That day and the months to follow, I learned a lot about relationships from our blossoming friendship.

> WHEN WE FOCUS ON OUR STRENGTHS, IT BREEDS COMPETITION. WHEN WE FOCUS ON OUR WEAKNESS, IT BREEDS COMMUNITY.

This brief exchange focusing on an area of weakness awakened something between the two of us. I began praying for my friend, calling him, checking on him, and even stopping in early one Sunday at his church before the services began. His reaction when I surprised him that morning was shocking. We prayed together in his office asking God to help us live victoriously and to help others do the same. The level of emotion and depth of relationship exchanged between us as a result of authenticity is almost indescribable. Vulnerability is God's secret ingredient to deeper, more meaningful relationships.

Nobody can be a great example until they stop trying to be a perfect example. Jesus is the only perfect example, and He clearly reveals that our access into His grace is through weakness rather than strength.

> And He said to me, "My grace is sufficient for you, for My strength is made perfect in weakness." Therefore most gladly I will rather boast in my infirmities, that the power of Christ may rest upon me. Therefore I take pleasure in infirmities, in reproaches, in needs, in persecutions, in distresses, for Christ's sake. For when I am weak, then I am strong. (2 Corinthians 12:9–10, NKJV)

The church must stop conning and start confessing if we are to become healthy and strong. Leonard Ravenhill said, "The greatest tragedy is a sick church in a dying world."[1] We are only as sick as we are secret. My experience in church over the years is to see people start their faith journey sincerely and honestly by getting real about their situation and

---

[1] http://www.ravenhill.org/.

recognizing their desperate need for Jesus. Once people get real, the church tends to try to make them good. When we try to make real people good, it produces presentation, and everybody gets confused. Jesus didn't spend time with good people when he came to the earth. Jesus spent time with real people.

Fake people aren't real, and real people aren't fake. Until we are willing to get real, then we will never discover what it is to be transformed into all God desires for us to become. True change is absolutely possible. True change is absolutely painful. It's painfully liberating to get vulnerable with someone you have learned to trust over time. This kind of relationship doesn't come easy and will take work.

It's worth the risk to be transparent. The alternative is to bottle up dysfunction, empowering the enemy to hold you back from all God desires for your life and legacy. When we settle for anemic relationships that lack true community, our lives become relationally impoverished. The tragedy of relational poverty is the life we never live and the difference we never make in other people's lives.

Recently, I was standing before a group of pastors and leaders sharing this idea. It was obvious as I spoke that God was moving on the hearts of these generals in God's army. Suddenly, I took them by surprise with a midmessage altar call asking those who were struggling with some kind of life-controlling addiction to stand to their feet. Ninety percent of these men and women quickly stood to their feet, many weeping as they stood. I'd like to give you that same opportunity midchapter right now. Mark your place and put this book down so you can reach out to a trusted friend about some area in your life that you want to take back from the enemy. Please don't read on until you've responded to whatever God is dealing with you about in your heart right now.

> *Father I pray in agreement that if two agree on earth*
> *as touching about anything, it will be done. If we*
> *confess our sins to each other and pray for each other,*
> *we will be healed. Thank you that as we obey your*
> *word and get vulnerable with others, not only are we*
> *impacted, but they are impacted as well. Amen.*

It is a huge myth in our culture that we can become spiritually mature on our own. As painful as it may be, we must take up our cross and be willing to suffer loss and die to ourselves to experience true resurrection power in our lives. There can be no resurrection if there is no crucifixion. We are created in the image of trinity/community of God. Therefore, we must stop being so intensely individualistic, or we will continually settle for less than God's best in our lives and in our world. By God's design, we can only grow so far alone and then we reach a place where it takes another human being to help get us to the next level. There are times in our lives when we must build a circle to break a cycle.

Having a Christian school ministry in our church with an enrollment of more than five hundred students has provided a lot of unique experiences over the years. In one instance, I was made aware of a fourth grader who was walking through some personal challenges in his home. I took an interest in this young man and began checking on him. About this time in his science class, the students began doing an experiment by planting a bean in a cup of dirt. In a brief time, the beans began sprouting up out of the dirt, that is, all of the beans except this young man's.

Finally after much progress in every single cup except for his, the teacher inquired with him, asking what he thought the problem was. With great frustration, he exclaimed, "I just don't know! Every day I pull back the dirt and look at the bean and it never seems to change." Whatever is uncovered simply will not grow. This is a principle that has stayed with me since I was made aware of that conversation. In all of our lives, if we will uncover the temptations, distractions, and frustrations, they simply can never take root and grow in our lives, keeping them from producing damaging and costly conclusions to our future.

Many times in my own life, I have wished for an easier way out other than painful transparency. God has a plan, and I pray that we will find enough courage in our hearts to walk this out together in community as God intends for us to do so. Lazarus was dead, and through Jesus, he was about to be brought into life.

> The dead man came out, his hands and feet wrapped with strips of linen, and a cloth around his face. Jesus said to them, "Take off the grave clothes and let him go." (John 11:44, NIV)

Notice that through Jesus, Lazarus came to life. However, it was through relationship with others that his grave clothes were removed. The more independent and disconnected we are, the more we spend our lives in grave clothes without experiencing true liberty and freedom. In our society, we tend to be overcommitted and unconnected. We are robbed of true community where deeper, more meaningful life and freedom are experienced.

In 2 Samuel 11, we read where David has an affair with another man's wife, has that man killed, covers it up, and then takes her as his own wife. He demonstrates how a man who is accountable to no one is capable of committing terrible sins that produce untold damage.

David was trying to move on with his life but was neglecting to deal with these terrible sins he'd committed. God sent Nathan to address this with David in the next chapter, and David immediately repents after the conversation. It wasn't that David couldn't see his sin. The fact was that David couldn't see his sin alone. In isolation, we are fully capable of justifying toxic, terrible attitudes and behaviors. We desperately need each other.

Seven times in Genesis chapter one, God says, "It is good." Of course, it is good! God is creating paradise, and there is no sin in the world. But we also learn that even in the perfectly structured atmosphere of paradise, it is still "not good for man to be alone!" No matter what kind of success we experience in this earth, it will never compare to perfect, sinless paradise. It will never be good for man to be alone. We've all heard and even bought into the phrase, "You can't take it with you." This only makes sense when you reduce what is valuable to the currency of this world. Relationship is the currency of God's kingdom, and we can take people with us. You can take "it" with you if you know what true treasure really is.

The world's system and the world's treasure is a cheap counterfeit to what is meaningful and true. The Bible describes our pursuit of these things as an adulterous relationship with the world.

Discussion Questions

1. Share a genuine and vulnerable relationship in your life and explain what it took to bring that about. If

you do not currently have a relationship like this in your life, begin to pray about who that person is, asking God to bring it about.

2. What are some ways you can effectively care for these God-given relationships in your life? Perhaps discuss how you list prayer needs to specifically be praying, how you purpose meaningful time together, how you encourage each other in the things of God, etc.

3. What is an area of dysfunction that you see trying to invade your life, and what are you doing to win that battle?

4. The world thinks "you can't take it with you." This limits the idea of riches to worldly wealth. You can take it with you when you realize true riches are authentic relationships. What is one thing you can do this next week to treasure true relationships in your life?

Scripture References for Further Reading and Study

2 Corinthians 12:9–10 (NKJV)
John 11:44 (NIV)
2 Samuel 11–12

Chapter 4

The Adulterous Woman

TRACY AND I'D been married for just two years. She was about to enter her second year of law school. I was a school principal at that time, and our lives were busy in many directions. Between my evening school activities and Tracy's intense demands in pursuit of her legal degree, our young and vulnerable relationship was neglected at times. Tension existed, and our conversations at home had drifted away from being warm and inviting. However, another woman I came across regularly was very warm, inviting, and even intriguing to me at times.

There were many evenings I found myself in the same house with my wife but feeling very alone as she would be studying, reading, writing, and preparing. Without even realizing it, my mind would begin drifting toward this other woman, thinking about when I might see her again. Over months, the stage was being set beautifully for what would have been the most destructive scene of my life. Something snapped in me as a conversational encounter with the other woman resulted in what I perceived to be an invitation for something more. She looked at me and said, "If only my husband could be more like you."

In this moment of conversation, I realized I was in an emotionally adulterous relationship. Adultery never happens when adultery happens physically. Adultery is the process of unhealthy emotional attachment and entanglement. I dismissed myself from the conversation and drove straight home to my wife. With all sincerity and all submission, I confessed openly to my wife that I'd been disconnected from her and woke up to the fact that I'd been inadvertently connecting emotionally with this other woman. Tracy spoke with grace, love, and forgiveness, as I was broken and tearful in my repentance to her.

Throughout the Bible, we find the analogy of adultery in regard to God's people, speaking of Israel's unfaithfulness. The ultimate conclusion of this adultery is seen in the book of Revelation: This title was written on her forehead: MYSTERY BABYLON THE GREAT, THE MOTHER OF PROSTITUTES AND OF THE ABOMINATIONS OF THE EARTH. I saw that the woman was drunk with the blood of the saints, the blood of those who bore testimony to Jesus. When I saw her, I was greatly astonished (Revelation 17:5–6, NIV).

Proverbs speaks of the woman of wisdom and the adulterous woman. We see in the wisdom of Proverbs how the adulterous woman is a seductive counterfeit, always projecting similarities that enhance the confusion. Both call out attracting guests. Wisdom calls from the tops of the heights of the city while the adulteress calls from a seat by the high places of the city. Both prepare a table for their guests. Wisdom puts something into you while the adulteress gets something out of you. Wisdom produces a rewarding life and lasting blessing while the adulteress produces short-term thrill, ending in regret and a diminished life.

James was addressing a group of people who were extremely devoted to their religious beliefs and would have never considered the physical act of adultery. However, his language clearly reveals that embracing the world with self-serving motives is embracing this other woman in the act of spiritual adultery.

"You adulterous people, don't you know that friendship with the world is hatred toward God? Anyone who chooses to be a friend of the world becomes an enemy of God" (James 4:4, NIV).

When we allow ourselves to be seduced by cultural ideologies, we prostitute our God-given gifts for self-fulfilling purposes. There is no question that we, as the modern-day church, have become emotionally entangled with what the Bible reveals as the adulterous spirit of the world. This woman is deceptive, and the affair always has a justifiable progression of steps and stages. One thing always leads to another.

> NONE OF US HAVE EVER MADE ANY MAJOR ACCOMPLISHMENTS OR MAJOR MISTAKES IN A MOMENT.

When something bad happens, gradually finally arrives then suddenly gets the blame. When something good happens, gradually finally arrives then suddenly takes the credit.

Everything in life has a progression. All of our beliefs are the result of an elaborately complicated process of various conclusions involving chemicals in the brain, emotions, and intellect. The good news is that one thing always leads to another for good as well as bad. We can make adjustments once we are made aware.

As a church leader over the years, I hadn't realized how I had gradually given myself to a love affair with success. I was driven to wake early and work late, and all of it was justifiable in my mind, given the eternal nature of my devotion. Unhealthy patterns with unhealthy pursuits produce an unhealthy church. Countless church conferences are readily available where polished ministry with increased church attendance is the central focus. Marketing strategies to get people to attend church were the primary focus of most conversations in my early years of pastoring our congregation. One day the Holy Spirit prompted me with a word that changed my entire perspective, "Stop trying to get the community into your church and start trying to get the church into the community."

This required a mind-set that adjusted toward building God's kingdom more than "my congregation." All of us would say that's our goal, but we must ask, "Do we have ministry expressions beyond the scope of that which benefits our congregational objectives as a personal reflection of our pursuit of success?" If our only expression of Christ is that which builds "our ministry," we are likely missing the point.

Clearly I was missing the point, so I began searching for ways to serve people and other organizations in our community. The greatest challenge was to rethink my priorities and the feelings of not having time for these "other things." I had to see a new perspective of generosity with my time. Now I was serving in places that did not benefit my pastoral objectives, so time invested could not be self-serving in that sense. Suddenly I was loving, serving, and giving without any ulterior motive behind my efforts, and it was refreshing.

Over time, healthy relationships were formed, and my role in our community became more pronounced. City officials began asking me to serve on boards, be involved in various community events, and speak in forums that were more business and community than church. I was astonished as the mayor of our city contacted me, saying he wanted to have me to speak at the community Christmas tree lighting held annually in the community, so I could bring a more focused message. He explained that he knew Christmas was about much more than a tree and invited me each year to share the true meaning of Christmas as hundreds of people from our community gather for this event.

As a Christian, I want to make a difference. Jesus demonstrated that the way to make a difference is to sacrificially make disciples. The adulterous woman always stands in the way of our sacrifice, offering shortcuts to more self-serving efforts. Institutional efforts are not the ultimate expression of the church that Jesus Christ died to empower. The Great Commission is an individual commission more than an institutional one. We must fight against the idea of reducing our mandate from fruitful Christians who make disciples to faithful Christians who attend church.

It's easier to respond to the adulterous woman's invitation to self-serving shortcuts offering comfort than the sacrifices required to pursue our call. This violates the sacrificial nature of our Savior and leaves the church filled with ineffective and unproductive consumers. When we are distracted by selfish motives, the resources of our lives become hijacked from the purposes of God. An anemic faith is revealed when we readily talk about the sacrifice of Jesus without much mention of the sacrifice He expects from us.

Many have reduced the Gospel to "good advice news." The aim tends to be a moral lifestyle promising a wonderful life on this earth as a result. The problem is that this is spiritual adultery promoting a love affair with the world! Jesus isn't the way to get the things you really love in this world. Jesus is the way! He must become the ultimate object of our affection. Our affections have been won over by the pleasures of this world in more ways than any of us care to admit.

We tend to live our lives in such a way that you would think Jesus said that he came that we might have and enjoy vacations and weekends. He said he came that we might have and enjoy life. True life! Not the adulterous counterfeit the world tries to offer. This is a life that loves, serves, and gives, making an impact in the lives of others every single day and making the choice to move from merely existing to truly living!

Pastor Dustin Bates said it well, "We live in a culture that has tried to tame Christianity into a self-serving religion." If we're not careful, we overemphasize the idea of being "attractional" as a church. When we do this, we exchange the priority of being deeply convicted for the pursuit of being greatly encouraged. The Great Commission of the church isn't "ya'll come"; it's "ya'll go!" Polished and professional ministry expressions have the ability to attract people and generate income. If we're not careful, all of this will lull us into a ministry model that can provide the appearance of success without effectively making disciples or reaching the lost.

Our approach has been to oversimplify complicated problems with persuasive talking points and enjoyable presentations that lack powerful and actionable expressions. This results in overpreaching and underreaching. Merely listening to sermons makes us more religious. Knowing what we ought to do is one thing. Doing what we know to do is another. The church of our generation is more educated than obedient. If we could learn to translate sermons into just a fraction of action we would truly change the world.

Awakening our selfless love for God's wisdom is abandoning our self-absorbed perspectives and the pursuit of this adulterous woman. True love is truly all about action. A young woman sitting on a blanket in a park would understandably react to a snake crawling on the blanket by screaming and running away. However, if that young woman were a mother with her infant on that blanket, the response would be very different. There is a secret skill set in every mother that would rival any trained ninja when it comes to protecting a child. Perfect love truly does cast out all fear, driving us to selfless and sacrificial places of grace and compassion for others. It's only this love for God and love for others that can effectively move us beyond our own self-absorbed passions. Those "adulterous people" we read about in James 4:4 are further explained in the previous verses: "You desire and you do not have...You do not have because you do not ask; you ask and do not receive because you ask wrongly, so you can spend it on your passions" (James 4:2–3, NET).

It's entirely possible to spend our lives passionately pursuing and possessing with wrong motives. The notion that God's greatest interest is to provide us with the best life this world has to offer is the most selfish religious conclusion possible. Our lives are part of a greater story of God's love for the world. We want Jesus to be passionate about our ideas and objectives. Are we willing to be passionate about his?

> IF WE DON'T DEVOTE OURSELVES TO THE GREATER PURPOSES OF LOVE, WE CONFINE OURSELVES TO A SELF-SERVING EXISTENCE. WE WERE BORN FOR MORE THAN THAT.

Discussion Questions

1. Describe a time in your life when you embraced the world with self-serving motives. What resulted from this situation?

2. What can you do over the next week to more self-lessly love, serve, and give into the lives of others?
3. Fruitful Christians make disciples. How are you doing this, and what are some things you can initiate to do this more effectively?
4. What is something you have taken away from a message you heard at church recently, and how can you put that into action?
5. It is easy to want Jesus to be passionate about our ideas. How can we more effectively be passionate about His?

Scripture References for Further Reading and Study

Revelation 17:5–6 (NIV)
Proverbs 7–8
James 4:2–4 (NIV, NET)

Chapter 5

Celebrities and Servants

TRACY AND I were expecting our first child. After Faith was born, Lexi came along just fifteen months later. Anticipating our new role as parents, we suddenly had an interest in healthy role models for our children. The latest Disney superstar at that time was in the Disney Channel spotlight. She was talking about her relationship with God in personal interviews, and I was taken by her Christian testimony. We were excited at the idea of pointing both Faith's and Lexi's attention toward Britney Spears as a wonderful example for our daughters to watch in their lives as they started growing up. No offense intended toward Britney, but things took a sudden change in her life. Shortly after great success, the news reported that she had shaved her head bald in a seemingly desperate state and checked herself into a drug rehab facility. It appeared that she lost herself in all the success at a very young age.

We regathered our efforts, now wanting to point the attention of our girls away from the example Britney was becoming. The timing was almost perfect as the next Disney superstar emerged just about the time the girls were old enough to be enamored with celebrities. Not only was this girl absolutely bold about her faith in Jesus Christ, but her father was right there by her side as a celebrity himself, giving glory to God. The girls first recognized her by her well-known character name on Disney as Hannah Montana. Miley Cyrus was a stellar example, and I even found myself being challenged by her convictions and standards at times, considering the world of phenomenal success she was living in. Somehow she seemed to be holding it all together and continuing to represent Christ. No offense to Miley either, but things in her life and career also took a sudden change. She quickly transitioned to a reputation of very sexually explicit performances.

None of us can even begin to understand what kinds of pressures and pain these and other superstars face in the world of outrageous success. On some level, we all have fans, friends, and foes. Fans make us think we're better than we are. Foes make us think we're worse than we are. Friends help us remember who we truly are. Fame thrusts a person into an overwhelming fan base that can quickly swallow them up, requiring them to become what will fascinate the people. To resist this would be to diminish the fan base, and fame has no room for those with diminishing interests of fans. The goal then becomes to do whatever you must to keep from losing ground in this pursuit of success and popularity.

The church of our generation has, in many ways, been evangelized by this celebrity culture. Creative ideas expressed in "attractional" church models can be very effective in getting attention and increasing a fan base. Jesus had a lot of fans at various times in his life and ministry. The ultimate pursuit was not to merely attract fans but rather to truly *make disciples*! Whatever we are willing to do to attract people, we must continue to do to keep them if we are to cultivate an effective fan base. If we're not careful, we devote ourselves to helping people fall in love with a clever speaker rather than the loving Savior.

As the lead pastor of Destiny, I've encouraged our team to see the value of being "attractional" correctly. This simply must be seen as a discovery component, which is incomplete but can be very helpful in fulfilling our commission to make disciples. The development component is the next step, where we take curiously interested people and introduce them to the cross of Jesus Christ. Clearly we must die if we want to live. It is indeed costly to be a true disciple of Jesus Christ. It costs what it costs, and it never goes on sale. There are no shortcuts, discounts, or easy ways to get through the cross to experience resurrection life.

Attracting a crowd doesn't make disciples, but it does make us feel successful, and therein lies the danger. There can be a sense of fulfillment by attending, being a member, and telling others about our awesome church, almost relinquishing our responsibility to personal ministry on a daily basis. Inviting people to experience the *institutional expression* our church family has created must never replace our *individual responsibility* to love, serve, and give into the lives of those who have been entrusted to our care in our home, at work, in stores and restaurants, etc. The reality is we can't go to church because we are the church. We gather as the church to more effectively be empowered to be the church in our everyday lives!

> WHEN WE COME TO CHURCH, OUR LIVES ARE ENRICHED. WHEN WE BECOME THE CHURCH, OUR WORLD IS ENRICHED.

The Great Commission, in many ways, has been reduced to "the great attraction." We must be careful never to reduce followers of Christ to mere attenders of church. Attenders love the celebrity culture, and as long as they are celebrated, they attend. When the celebration of their attendance lacks, there can be a drive to discover a new group of fans that will renew the celebration for their arrival and attendance.

The church of our generation has a message and a ministry that has largely been hijacked by this celebrity culture. The further we move in this direction, the more restless and bored the church tends to become. Restlessness and boredom are the result of smallness of purpose when we are not equipped to get past our own personal needs.

Recently, I was speaking to a group of pastors and said if the only expression of Christ is building our ministry, it is likely we are missing the point. Afterward, there were a few conversational reactions about my statement. I'd touched on the sacred pursuit of success, and it struck a nerve. Our hearts can drive us to succeed, but success in the wrong direction is a very dangerous threat to our destiny. The unseen motives of our hearts go unchecked if we only surround ourselves with fans that celebrate us. Fans celebrate us while foes criticize us. It's easy to migrate toward celebration especially when it medicates the pain of criticism and disappointment that foes can so often express.

True friendship brings a certain relational grace into our lives. Neglecting these healthy relationships produces isolation and moves us from the godly desire to be a servant to a worldly thirst of being a celebrity. True friends know how to celebrate us when we are right, discern us when we are wrong, and help us more clearly see this for ourselves. Vulnerability and transparency with a few honest

> WE WERE BUILT FROM GOD'S OPINION AND FOR GOD'S OPINION. WHEN MAN'S OPINION BECOMES OUR PRIORITY, WE DIMINISH OUR DESIGN.

relationships is vitally important to our lives and the wellness of the church. Healthy relationships bring a steady, loving challenge to die to our self-promoting pursuits so Jesus can be more readily lifted up!

It's absurd to strive to be validated by people who live about one century while neglecting the opinion of Eternal God! God designed us with character and strength to stand for who we are in Him. We were created in the image of an unchanging God, who is the same yesterday, today, and forever. When people shout praises, he remains the same. When people shout curses, he remains the same. When people welcome him to be part of the popular crowd, he remains the same. When people exclude him, he remains the same.

Jesus teaches in Mark 12:29 that the most important commandment is born from the reality that the Lord our God is one God. He's not one God to one person and another God to another person. His character is unchanging! My daughters and I enjoy watching bloopers and outtakes from movies. When an actor or actress breaks character, they've stopped expressing a role, and their true identity shows up. Until our character is rooted in the identity of God, we naturally produce many characters in many scenes of life, losing ourselves on the journey. Man was given dominion in the earth, but not until after he was created in God's image and likeness, being firmly rooted in God's character.

Then God said, "Let Us make man in Our image, according to Our likeness; let them have dominion" (Genesis 1:26, NKJV).

We were created to dominate. However, if we advance in dominion without being established in God's image according to His likeness, we easily lose ourselves in the pursuit of opportunities and accolades of humanity. If we're not careful, we can spend our entire lives refining and perfecting what we do rather than becoming who we truly are. When we are distracted by selfish motives, we get hijacked from the purposes of God. It takes focus and discipline to stop being the person people want us to be and start being the person God created us to be.

Whom we fear determines how we live. A servant culture is rooted in the fear of God and produces the pursuit of His recognition. The celebrity culture is rooted in the fear of man and produces the pursuit of man's recognition. Other people's opinions of us do not have to become our reality. Romans 2:11 in the Message Bible says, "God pays no attention to what others say about you. He makes up his own mind." God's purpose for us is always more powerful than other people's opinions of us.

My oldest daughter was twelve years old at the time. We were snuggling on the couch together looking at family pictures and family videos on my laptop. Somehow we ventured into a web search and stumbled upon my name being listed in some online radio broadcast. I didn't remember doing any interview with this person, so I clicked the link. I watched as my daughter processed an introduction to her father that neither of us expected. This radio personality had taken one of my recent sermons and debuted me as one of the top five heretics on his list. He would play brief portions of my message, take my comments out of context, and discuss the error of my ways.

We listened to several minutes of his commentary before I realized how upset my daughter was that somebody would say such terrible things about her daddy. I admit the sermon could have used some constructive criticism, but clearly, I am not the man he was describing me to be. Over the years, I've become connected with a number of pastors. I've observed how easy it is for leaders to be affected by so many people with so many opinions about how you should and should not do whatever you're doing. The more we live and lead according to the opinions of others, the less effective we will be.

Jesus taught about the danger of trying to keep everybody happy, saying in Luke, "Woe to you when all men speak well of you" (Luke 6:26, NIV).

Just because somebody writes our obituary does not mean we are obligated to die.

The best you is the relaxed you, and the relaxed you is only discovered when you truly rest in Him. The fear

> WE MUST NEVER WASTE OUR TIME TRYING TO EXPLAIN OURSELVES TO THOSE WHO ARE DEEPLY COMMITTED TO MISUNDERSTANDING US.

of man will prove to be a snare, but whoever trusts in the *Lord* is kept safe (Proverbs 29:25, NIV). Theology has been replaced by therapy, and the Good News has been replaced by good-advice sermons and series. The drive to keep people encouraged is born from the desire to keep people happy. Keeping people happy and encouraged keeps them coming back, but for what?

People lose sight of Jesus and themselves in the pursuit of successfully attracting people into their lives for whatever purposes they have in mind. If people are attracted to you because of your authenticity, the connection is natural. If people are attracted to you because of a person you're trying to be, you'll have to work at being something you're not in order to keep their attention.

Convictions are born from the sacrificial nature of the cross, and every person is required to take up their cross if they are to embrace Christ. The goal isn't to make bad people good. The goal is to make dead people live, but death is a choice, and then life results. This life is a mere seed to the eternal life that is available. As with any seed, it must die before it can become what it has the potential to become. To focus on enjoying the life of a seed is to miss the harvest God has in mind.

A.W. Tozer said, "The Church has surrendered her once lofty concept of God and has substituted for it one so low, worshiping men. Jesus wasn't addicted to affirmation nor should we be. This she has done not deliberately, but little by little and without her knowledge; and her very unawareness only makes her situation all the more tragic."[1]

Cultural ideas have trained us to pursue our potential rather than our call. Religious entrepreneurs with business plans have replaced the office of the pastor in many ways. The danger in it all is reducing the Jesus movement to Jesus motions that can more effectively be marketed to attract more consumers.

---

[1]   A.W. Tozer, *Tozer on the Almighty God: A 366-Day Devotional.*

Discussion Questions

1. In today's church world, why is it so easy to be more in love with a speaker than it is with our Savior?
2. It is very easy to fall into the trap of desiring man's opinion more than God's. Describe a time when you experienced this personally and explain how it affected your life.
3. Your life is perfectly equipped with the exact experiences your dreams require. The things you are passionate about are clues to your call. When looking at your experiences and your passion, what clues do you find about who God has called you to be?
4. Name a person whom you were drawn to because of their authenticity and describe the things you observed that communicated this to you.
5. What are the common struggles with simply being authentic in our lives, and how can we more effectively overcome those struggles?

Scripture References for Further Reading and Study

Mark 12:29
Genesis 1:26 (NKJV)

Romans 2:11 (MSG)
Luke 6:26 (NIV)
Proverbs 29:25 (NIV)

Chapter 6

Jesus Motions—
Jesus Movement

IN OUR DIGITAL world, we must learn to purpose human moments. We live in a world where conversation, interactions, and friendships have become more surface than substance, making them less authentic and almost counterfeit. The danger of anything counterfeit is how unnoticeable it is due to a close resemblance. I remember an episode of *Duck Dynasty* where the guys found ripe muscadine berries. After shaking the limbs so the berries would fall to the ground, they all began gathering the berries to take home. Uncle Si popped a few in his mouth as the reward for his labor. Suddenly he began spitting and trying to get the awful taste of this terrible berry out of his mouth. The other guys took great delight in pointing out that raccoons didn't know the difference between the kitchen where they eat and the bathroom where they relieve themselves. He'd actually tossed raccoon droppings in his mouth that looked so similar to the berries.

One of the greatest dangers of our faith is to mistake it for resembling religious behaviors that don't produce enrichment in any direction other than our own. There is a brand of Christianity that is popular in our world today that has effectively maneuvered our faith almost completely away from the needs of others. Our faith is a resource, and if the extent of this God-given resource is to merely believe for our own lives, this resource is being misappropriated and violating the loving, serving, giving nature of God. Western Christianity has largely reduced the idea of faith in God to the pursuit of a wonderful life for self, coupled with a disregard for others.

> WE MUST REFUSE TO MERELY GO THROUGH THE JESUS MOTIONS SO WE CAN BECOME THE JESUS MOVEMENT OF OUR GENERATION!

Biblical Christianity risked life and limb to further God's kingdom in the lives of others. Even people who rejected faith in Jesus were fascinated by the sacrificial love so commonly expressed from these Christians who were demonstrating such love and compassion. Eternal priorities bring enrichment of heaven into our fallen, depraved, and desperately selfish world.

God's plan is for you to have an amazing life not because you've pursued it for yourself but because you have provided it for others. This was the most basic and fundamental core belief of the first-century Church. In Paul's letter to the Christians in Ephesus, he addresses those who were stealing. Notice his address wasn't merely an exhortation to stop doing what was wrong so their lives would be better. He instructed these self-absorbed people in the church to get a job and make money specifically to do something useful for society, providing something for others in need.

> He who has been stealing must steal no longer, but must work, doing something useful with his own hands, that he may have something to share with those in need. (Ephesians 4:28, NIV)

The greatest tragedy of any person's sin is the life they never live and the difference they never make in the lives of other people. Our deepest sense of purpose is born from learning to be a part of other people's needs. Every place Jesus walked was enriched as God's kingdom was revealed through his life, love, and service to others. As Christians, we are the expression of God's kingdom that remains in the earth. We are hoping God will change our city, but God is hoping we will change our city. Interestingly, the Bible speaks of how Jesus is the light of the world (John 8:12) and how we are the light of the world (Matt 5:14). We are the Jesus movement to our generation as his light is revealed through our broken, surrendered, and available lives! Jesus has come—now we must go love, serve, and give as a lifestyle of service to Jesus and to the world He so desperately loves and wants to rescue!

When Christianity becomes the Jesus movement of any generation, entire societies suffer upheaval as cultural norms and ideologies are challenged and ultimately begin to shift. There is a sense of violence as God's kingdom begins to invade the earth. If you've ever been asleep in your room and somebody suddenly turned on the lights, you understand the reaction this can produce. Those who have not been enlightened by the love and the life of Jesus Christ are in a state of slumber and darkness, and the reaction to light can be extremely unpleasant at times.

Christianity invaded Rome by first becoming popular among the poor and destitute. The coming of a new kingdom and a new king was their hope. The Jewish authorities rejected Christ and the Roman authorities were threatened by the idea of a coming king. Rome suffered a devastating fire that burned for six days destroying more than half of the city. Many accused Emperor Nero saying he set the fire for his own amusement. Nero blamed the Christians conveniently aligning with concerns of revolt.

Many Christians were put to death in the most horrific ways imaginable for the amusement of the citizens of Rome. To Nero's surprise Christians would sing God's praises while being burned at the stake. Some Romans actually jumped out of the stands and rushed to these martyrs who were having this incredible experience of heaven on earth in terrible circumstances. In doing so these Romans were doomed to the same fate but were willing to accept the loss of this life to experience an obviously greater life that these Christians were experiencing with God in their final moments on earth.

The challenging question for us all is, how many people would be willing to die to have what they see in our experience with God? Is our relationship with Jesus compelling to our world? Jesus came, he lived, he died and he is risen! His resurrection and the release of God's power in God's people started a massive Jesus movement in the earth that continues today. The counterfeit of the Jesus movement is a mere Jesus motion that resembles the real movement yet is surface and lacks substance. We must refuse to merely go through the Jesus motions and choose to be the Jesus movement to our generation!

It is all too easy to slowly deviate from the true course of Christ. This slight deviation can go completely unnoticed, just a few degrees at a time, and that is what makes it so dangerous. In 1979, a passenger jet with 257 people on board left New Zealand for a sightseeing flight to Antarctica. Someone had mistakenly modified the flight coordinates by a mere two degrees. This error placed the aircraft twenty-eight miles east of their sightseeing destination. As they approached Antarctica, the pilots descended to a lower altitude to give the passengers a better look at the landscape. These experienced pilots had no way of knowing that the incorrect coordinates had placed them directly in the path of Mount Erebus, an active volcano that is more than twelve thousand feet tall.

The snow and ice covering the volcano surface, combined with the white of the clouds, made it appear as if they were flying over flat ground. By the time the instruments sounded the warning that the ground was rising fast toward them, it was too late. The airplane crashed into the side of the volcano, killing everyone on board. It was a terrible tragedy brought on by a minor error of only a few degrees.[1]

When the Jesus movement deviates by just a few degrees, it slowly becomes empty Jesus motions. This may seem like an innocent sightseeing trip at first but has the potential

---

[1]   Arthur Marcel, "Mount Erebus Plane Crash," www.abc.net. au/rn/ockhamsrazor/stories/2007/1814952.htm

to kill everybody on board. The church is called by God to evangelize the culture. However, the church of our generation has largely been evangelized by the cultural ideas that surround us. The Message Bible says it very well, revealing that this has been a challenge for God's people throughout the generations.

> Woe to those who live only for today, indifferent to the fate of others! Woe to the playboys, the playgirls, who think life is a party held just for them! (Amos 6:5, MSG)

So here is a quick test to see if your beliefs are more cultural ideology or biblical theology. One of the two verses below is correct, and one of them is incorrect:

> And Jacob worked seven years for Rachel and *they seemed to him like just a few days* because of his love for her. (Genesis 29:20, NIV)

Or

> And Jacob worked seven years for Rachel and *they seemed to him like forty years* because of his love for her. (Genesis 29:20, NIV)

This experiment reveals the cultural idea of infatuation as opposed to the biblical idea of love. I've asked this question now in dozens of forums, and the vast majority of people migrate toward the forty-year expression. If you're passionately in love but not able to be together for seven long years, infatuation and gratification define this as totally miserable, seeming like an eternity. True love joyfully and sacrificially does whatever it takes to experience and express something far more meaningful than self-fulfillment.

Dating relationships, as defined by our culture, move people in and out of relationships on the search for the perfect mate I want to have in my marriage. These ideas are born from self-centered infatuation and unfortunately are great practice for divorce. Perhaps this speaks of why divorce rates within the church resemble divorce rates outside the church in our generation.

Because Jacob was experiencing a mature and meaningful love rather than the counterfeit infatuation, his seven years of work seemed like just a few days. True love is willingly sacrificial. Infatuation is a counterfeit that is selfish and unable to delay gratification. Love is selfless and considers how my actions will affect this person I care about so deeply. There is nothing more painful than two selfish people trying to get happiness from each other. There is nothing more beautiful than two servants trying to give happiness to each other.

Marriage done well makes the other person happy. What "works" in a relationship is when you stop trying to make the relationship "work" for you and start loving, serving, and giving to somebody you love. Now that works! Remember, God wants you to have an awesome life, but the catch is, you're providing it for others rather than pursuing it for yourself. Clearly we see cultural and biblical ideas in conflict in this important area of life.

> As for me and my household, we will serve the Lord." (Joshua 24:15, niv)

Jesus's mission cost him his life because his mission was not this life. Your mission is bigger than the pursuit of a great life on earth. Let's refuse to just lift up our feet and be swept downstream by the swift current of our culture. The first-century church is clearly described in scripture as a Jesus movement of true disciples, which were turning their world upside down.

> They dragged [them] to the rulers of the city, crying out, "These who have turned the world upside down have come here too." (Acts 17:6, nkjv)

This expression of church isn't focused on "going to heaven" but rather fulfilling our commission to bring God's kingdom on earth as it is in heaven! The focus is God's power working in believers while in this world, demonstrating heaven in the earth! Largely, this idea has been sensationalized and completely misunderstood. The supernatural does not have to be spectacular. The supernatural power of a small act of kindness can easily be overlooked in our thrilling pursuit of spectacular expressions.

There is amazing power to be discovered in steady and common routines of life that can be so enriching. The table was in the holy place in the temple of the Lord communicating the sacred value of that which might seem so common.

Discussion Questions

1. The pursuit of happiness comes easy. What are some common ways we pursue a happy life for ourselves?
2. The pursuit of blessedness takes more work, requiring us to find ways to help others be happy and blessed. What are some consistent behaviors we can put into practice to do this more effectively?
3. Many Christians sincerely believe they are following Jesus Christ while their lives bear no resemblance to his at all. Why is this the case, and what is your advice to a person wanting to change this about their own life?

4. In reference to your marriage, or your most meaningful friendships if single: does your relationship more closely resemble two selfish people trying to be happy or two servants trying to serve each other? What adjustments can be made over this next week as a starting point to progress?

Scripture References for Further Reading and Study

Ephesians 4:28 (NIV)
John 8:12
Matthew 5:14
Amos 6:5 (MSG)
Genesis 29:20 (NIV)
Joshua 24:15 (NIV)
Acts 17:6 (NKJV)

Chapter 7

The Table

THREE PHRASES PEOPLE love the most: I love you! You're forgiven! Let's eat! These phrases are all about relationship. Everybody needs love, forgiveness, and connection to be healthy. Interestingly, this is discovered first in Christ. John 3 and Revelation 3 communicate how God loved the world (I love you), that he gave his only Son (you're forgiven), and Jesus stands at the door of our hearts, knocking. If we open the door, he comes in to eat with us and us with him (let's eat). We were created in the image of God, who is a community within himself as the Trinity. God created us with a design of community, giving us a deep sense of desire for community.

Jesus came and bypassed all order of religion that neglected relationship. Suddenly he's having meals with sinners. The Last Supper is a famous meal Jesus had with his disciples. Obviously, this was very common for Jesus to eat with his friends. After Jesus rose from the grave, one of the first things he did was eat a meal with his friends.

It is interesting that in the very beginning, we see a meal that was eaten without God ruining everything. Then in the concluding chapters of the book of Revelation, we find another meal: the marriage supper of the Lamb. Jesus is all about inviting the world to the table of the Lord, where we all become friends with God. Only through Jesus does the altar give access to the table.

> "[You] are presenting defiled food upon My altar. But you say, "How have we defiled You?" In that you say, "The table of the LORD is to be despised." (Malachi 1:7, NAS)

Notice how the altar and the table are eternally connected. The sacrifices on the altar are unacceptable when the table is defiled. The sacrifice on the altar is only pleasing if the table is in proper order. If you're disconnected from fellowship with God, your offering is not acceptable. The table of the Lord also involves His family. Jesus said in Matthew: "Therefore, if you are offering your gift at the altar and there remember that your brother or sister has something against you, leave your gift there in front of the altar. First go and be reconciled to them; then come and offer your gift" (Matthew 5:23–24, NIV).

Obviously, we all need to make room for relationships as our highest priority! Expressing our love, our forgiveness, and our time to connect over a meal all produce a demonstration of hospitality we find clearly revealed in Christ as our ultimate example. Jesus invited us to his table so we would invite others to our table.

> Don't just pretend that you love others. Really love them…get into the habit of inviting guests home for dinner. (Romans 12:9–13, NLT).

We live in a day where people live isolated and lonely lives. True Christianity introduces Jesus as the relational answer to this painful deficiency that exists in the lives of so many people. The pursuit of great influence in big platforms can cause us to miss the power of meaningful impact on personal levels.

God loved the world in big ways, but it wasn't until He embraced humanity in his smallest posture of intimate existence that the world could forever be changed. We tend to express grand statements of big love in the songs we sing and the sermons we celebrate. It's not until we take a small posture of intimate connection with people on a personal level that lives will be changed. People ministering to people on a personal level will truly change the world.

Jesus spoke to masses of people very rarely, and these large groups were remarkably fickle. The same crowd who wanted to celebrate him was the same crowd who later wanted to crucify him. It was the very few whom he spent his most intimate time with who turned their world upside down.

After many years of serving his congregation, Pastor Simon came to his final Sunday. He had given his life to ministry and was now entering into the next season of life. His words carried incredible weight and spoke of legacy after decades of sacrificial ministry. He skillfully used his words like an accomplished artist to paint a masterpiece as his concluding message that day. The church family responded by coming forward, embracing, weeping, and laughing, offering their love and appreciation for his years of faithful service to their families. He fully expected to hear accolades of gratitude for all the wonderful messages he'd preached. Something very interesting happened that day. Not one person thanked him for a sermon. Dozens and dozens of specific situations were voiced as this church family thanked him for being there personally in moments of crisis, helping in times of need, and making a difference in the lives of individuals.

Pastor Simon experienced an ocean of comments thanking him for the hands and feet of his ministry. Not one person ever even mentioned the mouth of his ministry. It wasn't that the mouth wasn't important congregationally because it was. The simple truth of ministry is that individual influence is more powerful than institutional influence. At the core of our faith in and love for Jesus Christ, the most important objective is to love people personally just like Jesus does.

Paul wrote to the Corinthian church, saying in 1 Corinthians 4:20, "The kingdom of God is not a matter of talk." If we amputate the hands and feet from the Body of Christ and keep only a big mouth, we settle for making a point when we're called to make a difference.

LAZY COMPLAINING IS MUCH MORE CONVENIENT THAN LOVING INFLUENCE. THIS IS A MISAPPROPRIATION OF OUR VOICE AND OTHER PERSONAL RESOURCES.

The enemy loves to trick us into squandering away our ability to effectively address injustice by giving ourselves to self-absorbed rants. Don't just tell us what you're against. Show us what you're about. Help us reimagine a better story.

People caring for people makes the world a better place. People complaining about people makes the world a bitter place. The oversimplification of life's very complicated problems is very damaging and divisive. Nobody can have all the facts, but somehow it's very easy to feel completely confident that we have all the answers in our passionate discussions. This shows up very clearly in America every four years, when the right political candidate resonates with our ideas, justifying the positions we have believed to be right all along.

One of the greatest contributors to angry religious arguments is that preaching has become the emphasis of our churches rather than the catalyst for personal ministry. Gathering to embrace the teaching of God's Word has always been part of God's plan for worship. The New Testament church was born as Peter preached to masses of people. Once the multitude was converted, they didn't indoctrinate the converts with talking points. Disciples invested in them, helping them becoming disciples who cared for others, sacrificially following the example of Jesus loving, serving, and giving into the lives of other people. We must purpose to invest ourselves in the lives of others in a very intimate and intentional way. This is how we make the most of our eternal assignment in these temporal years.

Preaching serves the purpose of empowering the church to perform the work of the ministry. Our city will be transformed by our Christian hospitality over tables long before it will be transformed by pastors preaching in their pulpits. The doctrine of Christian hospitality is something that is required of pastors in 1 Timothy 3 and Titus 1. We see this is required of Christians in Romans 16. where Paul commands the whole church there to practice hospitality. Hospitality is welcoming people into your life and into your home to sit together at your table, treating them in a gracious way, expressing love through friendship.

Jesus came teaching in Matthew 10:7 that the kingdom of God is at hand, revealing that life's greatest treasures are within our reach. In a world that is overcommitted and underconnected, it is easy to miss out on the deeper, more meaningful treasures of life. The essence of hospitality is something that comes very naturally from within our families rather than something we fabricate in efforts to evangelize.

Don't underestimate or underuse the power of the kitchen table! My wife and I had our first date over a meal. Coming together for a meal has become a sacred place of common connection in our marriage and now for our family. The transforming power of hospitality has a profound influence on our children as we prepare food together, set the table together, have a meal with conversation on every level of life, and then clean up together. Sometimes the conversation is deep and meaningful. Sometimes the conversation is light and humorous. Always the place of the table is a safe place where everybody can be themselves, and we get to know each other through the seasons of life. It shouldn't surprise us to discover that countries with strong food cultures typically have a strong family culture.

The Bible describes how Jesus prepares a table for us in the presence of our enemies. Perhaps the idea behind this is to sit with us and connect with us according to His ways, protecting us from wrong ways of thinking represented as our enemies. Studies show that the more often families eat together, the less likely kids are to smoke, drink, do drugs, be depressed, and consider suicide.[1] Also, they are more likely to do well in school, delay having sex, eat their veggies, learn big words, and know which fork to use. It's this regularly shared meal, not holiday feasts, that anchors the family. Some nights, it is a fast-paced eat-and-run experience when everybody at the table is thinking about other places they truly need to be. However, the pattern of the table produces something profound in our lives and sometimes provides a lingering experience where everybody gets caught up in the conversation and no one feels stupid, shy, or ashamed as conversation erupts. This is where you get a glimpse of the power of a family at the table.

The table was in the holy place in the temple of the Lord, communicating the sacred value of that which might seem so common. It would serve us well to remember that Jesus was so common that it caused many to miss the sacred, powerful, and profound revelation He was carrying for the world. Perhaps we've been having conversations with our world through a bullhorn that need to be happening around a coffee table. If we're not careful, we can

---

[1] Sarah Klein, "8 Reasons to Make Time for Family Dinner," http://www.cnn.com/2011/10/25/living/family-dinner-h/.

easily revert to a bullhorn agenda even while sitting at the coffee table.

Everybody has a system of beliefs, which are born out of personal positions we have derived in our way of thinking. These beliefs are fortified with emotion and branded with experiences, producing arguable conclusions from which we have made many of life's decisions. Some people are more gracious and loving about their arguable conclusions than others. The application of scripture introduces God's point of view to our conclusions, fortifying our positions as truly sacred. If we're not careful, we cultivate talking points more than we cultivate compassion. We must focus on the transforming love of Christ rather than the destructive power of religion.

Wisdom doesn't attend every argument to which she is invited. We must learn to let love be our argument. It will leave our enemies speechless. When Christians get more interested in winning arguments than loving people, they are simply no longer like Jesus. Having the right argument with the wrong attitude makes you dead right, and nobody wants to be dead, right?

Love and compassion embraces people without feeling obligated to change their point of view. This allows us to discover the power of the table in a variety of relationships. Let your love be louder than your agenda! I love you. You're forgiven. Let's eat.

Discussion Questions

1. What are some ways you minister to people on a personal level?
2. What are some ways others have ministered to you on a personal level over the years?
3. What are some other examples of how true disciples invest themselves in the lives of others in an intimate and intentional way?
4. On a scale of 1–10, where would you rate yourself in hospitality, welcoming people into your life, into your home to sit together at your table, and treating them in a gracious way, expressing love through friendship? What can you begin to do to improve your score by at least one point?
5. Is eating together at the table a common practice in your home? If so, how have you accomplished this? If not, what needs to happen so you can accomplish this?

Scripture References for Further Reading and Study

John 3
Revelation 3
Malachi 1:7 (NAS)

Matthew 5:23–24 (NIV)
Romans 12:9–13 (NLT)
1 Corinthians 4:20
1 Timothy 3
Titus 1
Romans 16
Matthew 10:7

Chapter 8

Jesus Is the Messiah

POWERFUL AND COMPELLING stories are rarely born from the best of times. The greatness of any movie is discovered in the deep connection that takes place between our hope for something better and a story line that provides a comeback of some kind that is against all odds. The Champion, Apollo Creed, stages an easy fight with an unknown fighter who had no chance to win. Rocky captures our hearts with hope for anybody who feels hopeless in any area of life. Hope doesn't come from watching great people perpetuate an impossible level of success. Hope comes when we are inspired to move beyond the realm of impossibility and begin thinking in a greater realm from the greater dimension of possibility. This is where our imperfect, impossible, and even dysfunctional story becomes a prime candidate for God to use to inspire the world around us!

God is such an incredible writer and master at theatrics that he knows how to lower the light at just the right time when it looks like it's over. It looks like you've given everything and experienced no reward for your suffering. God knows how to dim the lights and leave everybody watching in a place of absence of anticipation, and ALL OF A SUDDEN, the lights explode to full power with the orchestra full force as the final act upsets the moment of darkness and disappointment! This is the story of an older couple unable to have children for more than two decades, even after God promised Isaac. This is the story of the Red Sea before you and Pharaoh's army behind you before the waters part. This is the story of the walls of Jericho that are the strongest, most intimidating walls imaginable that are about to fall! This is the story of a giant who scoffs at a shepherd boy who is about to be made into a national hero. This is the story of a virgin who will give birth simply because God says so. This is the story of Jesus's dead body in the tomb with no hope left, yet still He lives!

The Bible is littered with stories of impossible odds that take place in the lives of unlikely people doing extraordinary things. FAITH MAKES THINGS POSSIBLE, NOT EASY. God has continually proven over the generations that he does his best work in the realm of impossibility as we are drawn into a place where only he can get the glory. If we're not careful, we work at completely avoiding this realm in efforts to present something unrealistically amazing about our journey and about our lives. Your mistakes are part of your message.

You can't effectively *mentor* others if you don't allow *men* to *tour* your successes and your failures. Don't hide the scars God wants to use.

Tracy and I went shopping for a leather couch. As we were looking, we noticed a distressed leather couch. There was a tag on this beautiful couch that said something like, "All of the markings, scarring, and discolorations on this product are normal and enhance its natural beauty." As I read this, I pondered how a tag on our lives might read. Perhaps it would say, "This person is not faulty or damaged. All the markings, scarring, and blemishes are normal and enhance the humanity and authenticity of a life lived in pursuit of the purposes of God."

The idea of being a great example is probably one of the most confusing ideas in our faith. YOU CAN NEVER BE A GREAT EXAMPLE UNTIL YOU STOP TRYING TO BE A PERFECT EXAMPLE. The original sin was the pursuit of perfection. Adam and Eve bought into the lie that they could become like God. The Fall of humanity was born from the appetite for perfection, and then the great cover-up began. Great confusion in the church today results from the pursuit of perfection and the covering of mistakes. The Bible teaches us to confess our faults to each other and to pray for each other as a means of accessing God's healing and restoring power (James 5:16). Religious confusion rejects this notion of vulnerability in order to protect and project a certain image.

It's easy to allow our concern for our reputation to mask our mistakes and cover disappointing decisions we've made. People desperately need to know how eager God is to move us past our history by introducing us to our destiny. It is truly selfish to hide our mistakes from humanity. God openly reveals the mistakes of his family throughout the generations, inspiring us to remove our masks and embrace his grace no matter what the circumstances of our lives have been.

The New Testament begins with Matthew's account of the lineage of Jesus, and all the dirty laundry is disclosed right up front. Rahab, who was a prostitute, is right there in the lineup as a grandmother several generations back in the lineage of Jesus. Jesus had a grandfather in his lineage that had an affair with Bathsheba and tried to cover it up by murdering her husband who was his faithful friend. Throughout scripture, this theme of transparency and full disclosure is clear. Abraham was too old to have a child. Leah was unattractive. Joseph was abused and forgotten. Moses stuttered. Jonah was disobedient and slow to finally respond. Elijah was suicidal. Peter was hot-tempered. Martha was a worrier. Thomas had his doubts, yet Jesus never scolded him but rather provided the evidence he required to believe. It seems the entire lineage and everybody surrounding it is one huge mess. Perhaps that's why we know Jesus as the "Messiah" who takes our mess and turns it into a message.

Imperfection in your life is helpful to others. Stop covering up what God is trying to use to demonstrate his love and grace. Our world desperately needs to know God isn't mad at them, but rather, he's mad about them!

"God chose the foolish things of the world to shame the wise; God chose the weak things of the world to shame the strong" (1 Corinthians 1:27, NIV). The Greek word for foolish is *moros*, from which we get our English word *morons*. God's not looking for the most amazing people in the world who have it all together to show how awesome He is. God's looking for morons so he can demonstrate how much he can accomplish with so little to work with! This means we are all qualified, and God goes to great lengths to demonstrate and reveal this in his Word.

The twelve sons of Israel were born out of arguably the most dysfunctional family in the history of the world. Each child born was given a name with a meaning to spite family members. Leah was the wife Jacob never wanted, and this obviously produced great pain in her life. She had Jacob's first son, giving him a name to express her pain, naming him Reuben, meaning *he's seen my misery*. She then had Levi, meaning *at last, my husband will be attached to me*. Her third son she named Judah, meaning *I'll praise the Lord*. Rachel brought in a maid named Bilhah since she wasn't getting pregnant, and when she conceived and had a son, Rachel named him Dan, meaning *God has vindicated me*! Bilhah conceived again, and Rachel named this son Naphtali, meaning *I have struggled with my sister*!

Leah wouldn't be outdone, so she invited a handmaid of her own, Zilpah, into the party. Zilpah's first son was named Gad, meaning *what good fortune*. Her next son was named Asher, meaning *how happy I am*! Leah then had two more sons, naming them Issachar, meaning *God has rewarded me*, and Zebulun, meaning, *now I will be honored*. Finally, Rachel had a son, naming him Joseph, meaning *may he add to my life*. The final son was born to Rachel, who died during childbirth, naming him Benoni before she died, meaning *son of my trouble*. However, Jacob intervened, renaming him Benjamin, meaning *son of my right hand* so he wouldn't be known as one who brought death but rather one who has life.

The truly fascinating thing about this dysfunctional progression is that it tells a story that speaks of our lives. This is actually the progression of salvation that all began when we were lost: *Reuben,* "he saw our misery," and then through Christ, we became *Levi,* "attached" to God. We began to *Judah,* "praise" God and *Dan,* He "vindicated" us. We learned that salvation involves the *Naphtali,* "struggle" as part of maturity, but as we move beyond the struggle, we experience *Gad,* "good fortune" and *Asher,* "happiness" as God *Issachar,* "rewards" us, and *Joseph,* "adds to" our lives. We are in Christ who hung on the cross as Mary watched *Benoni,* "son of my trouble," but the Father raised him up, saying no, he'll not be known by death but rather for life as *Benjamin*, the "son of my right hand!"

God didn't hide any of the dirty laundry in the Bible. God's love in our messed-up lives is the message of Gospel. This vulnerability and authenticity causes Christianity to stand in a class of its own as no other religion allows its heroes to be exposed in their expression of scripture. Clearly Christianity doesn't allow our issues to be our excuses. God has always used dysfunctional people. You are not merely carriers of a message. You are the message. Others can be encouraged when they see your limitations in the same way we find encouragement by seeing these mighty men and women of God who made mistakes.

In the midst of our dysfunction and in the midst of our pain, we must never forget that God is at work!

So many times, God surrounds us with people who need to hear our story, so our history never becomes their destiny. Whatever we face, we must walk it out and help others do the same using our hurt to bear fruit. Pain becomes purpose when hurt produces fruit. Pain becomes poison when hurt produces hate.

> OFTENTIMES, OUR DEEPEST PAIN INTRODUCES US TO OUR GREATEST PURPOSE.

We must guard against using our wounds as weapons to justify our revenge.

He comes alongside us when we go through hard times, and before you know it, he brings us alongside someone else who is going through hard times so that we can be there for that person just as God was there for us (2 Corinthians 1:4, MSG).

Many times, our best ministry is just on the other side of our worst tragedy. EVENTS OF OUR LIVES MAY EXPLAIN US, BUT THEY DON'T HAVE TO DEFINE US.

Sometimes we settle not because we can't achieve it, but because we feel we don't deserve it. When we were born, our identity was born into dysfunctional, fallen Adam. When we were born again, the risen Christ redeemed us, giving us a new identity in Him who is at the right hand of the Father.

Our ability to live and our ability to love are limited to our willingness to manage pain. The key in all of this is to focus more on the purpose than we do on the pain. WE ARE ALL INCLINED TO IDENTIFY WITH DYSFUNCTION, BUT WE ARE DESIGNED TO IDENTIFY WITH DESTINY.

Some people in the Bible are namelessly known by their dysfunction. There is "the crippled man," "the woman with issue of blood," "the man with a withered hand," and blind Bartamaeus who did get a name but dysfunction still defined his identity before his name said who he was. You have no right to disqualify somebody God has chosen—not even yourself. God didn't love you back. He loved you first! Jesus took hold of our lives to move us beyond dysfunction to a place of destiny!

We must choose daily to identify with our purpose more than we identify with our pain or we exchange our destiny for our dysfunction. Moving on is like crossing the monkey bars. If we don't let go, we can't move forward. Through the ages, generations of people have viewed King David as a mighty man of God. Yet we read in 2 Samuel 11 when David committed adultery with Bathsheba and then murdered her husband to cover it up. Eleven chapters later, in life David writes these words as if he'd never made any mistakes:

> The LORD rewarded me for doing right; he compensated me because of my innocence. For I have kept the ways of the LORD; I have not turned from my God to follow evil. For all his laws are constantly before me; I have never abandoned his principles. I am blameless before God; I have kept myself from sin. The LORD rewarded me for doing right, because of my innocence in his sight. (2 Samuel 22:21–25, NIV)

How could David say such a thing when he'd made such horrible mistakes? David's mistakes didn't disqualify him from being restored by God. Perhaps it's for this same reason, generations of people have not disqualified him as a mighty man of God. The embrace of grace has the capacity to introduce us to a destiny beyond any level of disappointment. The problem is typically, we tend to stand feeling rigidly undeserving when we are embraced by grace. We've all experienced that awkward moment of extending an embrace to a person who doesn't respond with the same expression. David didn't do that. He responded to grace. He moved beyond his mistakes though they left him where he did not want to be at that point in his life.

Maybe you've made mistakes and aren't where you want to be. Your past doesn't have the power to take away your future if you will simply keep writing a story that will inspire others beyond disappointment to destiny!

Discussion Questions

1. What are the few things we do commonly to protect our image? Think about a social setting where you are meeting people as you respond.
2. Describe a time you allowed your desire to present a certain image that kept you from being yourself.

3. How can you allow your mistakes to be used for the greater purposes of God? Are there any examples of how you are already doing this?

4. Do people commonly see God as mad at them or mad about them, and why? What can we do to help with this perspective in our immediate environments?

5. It is so easy to miss our future because we are absorbed with something in our past. What advice could you give somebody who simply struggles with letting things go in their history, keeping them from so much in their destiny?

Scripture References for Further Reading and Study

James 5:16
1 Corinthians 1:27 (NIV)
2 Corinthians 1:4 (MSG)
Genesis 29–30, 35:18
2 Samuel 22:21–25 (NIV)

Chapter 9

We All Have a History, We All Have a Destiny

WHAT A PRIVILEGE to meet John Maxwell personally. I've read his books and listened to his teaching on leadership for years. I'd been invited to speak at a few breakout sessions at a larger conference, and John Maxwell was the main speaker. Standing in the speakers' lounge together, I took the opportunity to introduce myself. It struck me how many times John rehearsed my name in the next few minutes of casual conversation. Later on that day, John walked by and called me by name once again. I felt privileged. John Maxwell knew my name!

Over the next week, I thought about having had the opportunity to meet John and how inspiring it was. There really was something about the fact that he remembered my name that caused me to feel a little better about me.

The very next week, I received the CD of the month I'd been receiving for quite some time from my subscription to Maximum Impact, Maxwell's offer to better equip leaders.

This CD was different. As I opened the package, I felt a sense of personal connection to my friend John Maxwell, having met him personally and of course realizing that he remembered my name. Driving across town, I popped in that CD to hear this month's leadership principle. As the CD began to play, my friend John opened with this statement, "Today I'd like to share what I call the postman principle. Learn the names of insignificant people. It will mean a lot to them."

Needless to say, I found it hilarious that I'd been such a perfect illustration of Mr. Maxwell's teaching point on how he effectively reached the "insignificant people" who happened along his path. The funny thing was that he was totally right. For some reason, it had meant a lot to me. It is impossible to truly comprehend the depth of insecurity that exists in all humanity, driving us to seek approval, affirmation, and anything to help us medicate the pain of our past and stimulate hope for our future.

Opportunities, success, and affirmation tend to provide a sense of discovering significance. Disappointment, discouragement, and frustration tend to provide a sense of diminished significance. When we can settle the issue of God's love for us, we will finally stop living for the praise of others. This is the place where the disapproval of our critics no longer slows us down.

Just relax, and you will be revealed correctly. Anything else is a presentation, and this compulsion to do so is typically born from the lie that our history has somehow diminished our destiny. Nothing could be further from the truth. With Jesus, destiny outweighs history, purpose outweighs pain, the crown outweighs the cross, hope outweighs hardships, and grace outweighs shame! Blessing always out-

> LEARNING TO LIVE FROM GOD'S APPROVAL FREES US FROM STRIVING TO LIVE FOR MAN'S APPROVAL.

weighs burden because where there is sin, there is always much more grace, as Paul explains in Romans 5.

Regardless of where you've been or what you've done, you can be completely restored to the greater purposes of God or else, the sacrifice of Jesus was not more powerful than your mistakes. Former perspectives blind us from fresh perspectives if we focus on our history more than our destiny. Only fools allow themselves to continually be defined by their history. Be awakened to God's purposes today, an¹ be defined by your destiny! Stop judging your¹ past; you don't live there any more.

Peter tells Jesus in Mark 14 how his love and devotion is greater than his desire to live. Peter boldly proclaims that even if he must die, he will stand with Jesus to the very end. In this same chapter of life, Peter fails Jesus by falling asleep when Jesus needed him to pray and, then shortly after this, was completely ashamed after denying Christ. Peter must have felt so fascinated to be used by God. Not when the rooster crowed, but on the day of Pentecost soon thereafter! Recover from your mistakes!

It's impossible to embrace all God has for your future when you keep clinging to your past. The redemption of your past may be exactly what other people need to see in order to believe there is hope for their situation as well.

When I Google the word *Samaritan*, a host of websites dealing with assisting people in need filled the page. This idea of a "good Samaritan" is starkly contrasted to the idea of a Samaritan in Jesus's day. The Jews had no dealings with Samaritans and even hated them, calling them "dogs" or "half-breeds." Samaritans were descendants of Abraham through Joseph's sons, Manasseh and Ephraim, who, over time, began intermarrying with Gentiles. Nobody, including them, saw them as "good." Only Jesus can take a shameful name characterized by compromise and turn it into a name that is known by His loving compassion.

John 4 tells the story of the Samaritan woman Jesus asked for water and then told her about living water. Jesus didn't focus on her mistakes or the mistakes of her legacy. His focus was on the living water rather than the things that had kept her from it. Jesus always sees more in us than we do. No matter what the history and legacy of your life may be, Jesus changes everything! In just one conversation, this Samaritan woman gained understanding more quickly than Jesus's most faithful followers. Suddenly, she saw something in herself that nobody else could see. Moving past disqualification that had branded her, she was used mightily by God. After encountering Jesus, she brought transformation to an entire city!

Jesus is always addressing these issues of hateful disqualification to help us reimagine a better future. When Jesus explained the parable of the good Samaritan, he was expressing something very volatile in the culture of his day. He was describing how these compromising Samaritans could be more in touch with God's loving and generous nature than the religiously respected priests and Levites.

THE GREAT I AM CAN TURN ANY HAS BEEN INTO A WILL BE!

So you've made mistakes and may not be where you want to be. It is never too late to be what you might have been. Your decisions determine destiny. Where you are only defines your starting point. Don't let it bother you when people say they knew you. Unless they know you now, they don't know you well. History is where we discover the place we learned life's lessons. Destiny is where we discover a place to apply what we've learned. We must refuse to let our history rob us of our destiny!

Paul says he is pressing on to take hold of everything Jesus had in mind when he took hold of Paul. "I press on to take hold of that for which Christ Jesus took hold of me" (Philippians 3:12, NIV). Jesus took hold of you for a purpose, and the struggles of your past are part of your future assignment.

God never wastes a single hurt in our lives. It is impossible to embrace all God has for your future when you keep clinging to your past. Rehearsing the pain of the past hinders our ability to freely love others, as pain has the power to slowly redefine our perspective, producing sensitivity and reactions.

The car accident I had when I was seventeen years old was branded deeply into my emotions and thoughts. For the next year, any time I heard screeching tires or the impact of an accident, I became short of breath and almost emotionally distraught for a moment. If we're not careful, we rehearse the mistakes we've made or the mistakes others have made that have impacted us, and our reactions become so strong they overpower our ability to respond.

Religious confusion abounds when the ability to love is hindered. Our ability to forgive ourselves is directly connected to our ability to forgive others. Our ability to forgive others in our past is directly tied to our ability to forgive others in our future.

If we aren't careful, we can allow our own attitudes to rob us of God's perspective. When we nurse hurt, we grow poison. It's entirely possible to wake up one day surrounded by people we've infected with complaints, rather than those we've inspired with our love.

WHEN DISAPPOINTMENT DRIVES OUR DOCTRINE, ACCUSATION TAKES CONTROL.

Pain naturally produces a reaction, and that reaction is rarely peaceful, loving, or good. On a few occasions, I've had the misfortune of missing the nail and finding my thumb when swinging a hammer. Suddenly a chemical tsunami is released in the brain, as it does its job communicating to the body that something hurts, and an array of emotional reactions result. Life is full of these moments, and emotional pain has the same ability to produce outrageous reactions. When we focus on the pain, we are prone to miss the point. Amy Carmichael wrote, "If you are filled with bitterness and jolted your bitterness will come out. It is not the fault of the person who jolted you."[1]

Whisper was an amazing dog. We gave him his name because he wouldn't make a sound when he was a puppy. But boy, did that change. Whisper was a white fluffy American Eskimo, a member of the high-strung spitz family. He was always so loyal and very gentle with our family, even with our small children who put him to the test at times. However, one day, he was injured, and when I rushed to his aid, my reaction was to pick him up. As I picked him up, I contributed to his pain, and he sunk his teeth into my forearm. Tears were streaming down my cheeks as I tried to help him, and the pain from the bite was not the source of my tears. Whisper would recover and later be fine, but I would never forget the uncharacteristic reactions we are all capable of when we are in pain.

The more we focus on our pain, the more self-absorbed we become. The more self-absorbed we become, the less loving and caring we will be.

---

[1] Carmichael, Amy. *If* (Fort Washington: Christian Literature Crusade), 46.

Discussion Questions

1. What are some things others have identified or seen in you that you've not really identified or seen?
2. What are some things you've seen in yourself that you feel others may not have noticed or identified?
3. On a scale of 1–10, how hard are you on yourself about mistakes you make? How do you think this affects the way you form opinions and perspectives of others?
4. What are some ways a person's own attitude can easily rob them of God's perspective?
5. Describe a time you allowed pain to produce a reaction in your life. Explain how that affected your relationship with others.

Scripture References for Further Reading and Study

Romans 5
Mark 14
John 4
Philippians 3:12 (NIV)

The Trendy Trinity

THE *New York Times* reported research published by the United Nations[1] stating world hunger could be solved for $30 billion a year. CNN Health estimates eighty million Americans go on diets every year, spending more than $30 billion on programs and products.[2] There is a certain injustice about the population of one nation spending the exact amount of money to fight that nation's gluttony that would solve starvation in all the nations of the world.

[1]   Elisabeth Rosenthal and Andrew Martin, "UN Says Solving Food Crisis Could Cost $30 Billion," June 4, 2008, http://www.nytimes.com/2008/06/04/news/04iht-04food.13446176.html?_r=0.

[2]   Tracy Minkin, "The Top 10 Healthiest Diets in America," December 29, 2008, http://www.cnn.com/2008/HEALTH/12/29/healthiest.diets/index.html?_s=PM:HEALTH.

The sense that somebody should do something about this travesty is reinforced to learn further information about how the three richest people in the world control more wealth than the poorest forty-eight nations.[3] Why don't the rich people do something about this? Perhaps the more pertinent question to our lives is, "Who are the rich people?"

Standing before our congregation one morning, I asked them to do something very simple, "Raise your hand if you're rich." As you're reading this book, I'd like to ask you the same question. Are you rich? The answer to this question can be discovered in another question: "What is rich?"

A Gallup survey was conducted, asking people, "What is rich?"[4] People making $35,000 per year said those making $75,000 per year were rich. If you ask somebody making $75,000 per year, they wouldn't think they were rich. The average American polled thought people making $150,000 per year was rich. Readers of *Money Magazine* were polled, and that group of people thought having one million dollars in liquid assets would be rich. It seems as if the idea of

---

3   "Consumption by the United States," Washington State University, accessed June 20, 2014, http://public.wsu.edu/~mreed/380American%20Consumption.htm.

4   "2015 Survey of Affluence and Wealth," Time Inc. (TIME: NYSE) and YouGov.

being "rich" is a fleeting notion no matter how much money or assets we acquire. These studies indicate the desire for more exists on every level of financial accomplishment, leaving our society completely incapable of defining what rich truly is.

Surely we could conclude that at least the top 1 percent of wealth earners in the world could take it upon themselves to do something to help others in need. The Charles Koch Foundation once released a commercial revealing that an annual income of $34,000 puts a person among the wealthiest 1 percent in the world. If this is the case, then a very modest household income in America positions us better off financially than 99 percent of the people in the world, bringing a great deal of responsibility.

Once I heard about four people named Everybody, Somebody, Anybody, and Nobody. Something needed to be done, and Everybody was sure that Somebody would get it done. Anybody could do it, but Nobody did. Somebody got angry because this was clearly Everybody's responsibility. Anybody could do it, but Nobody realized that Everybody thought Somebody else would get it done. The conclusion was that Everybody blamed Somebody when Nobody did what Anybody could have done.

Religious confusion happens when the trendy trinity holds us captive to the selfish pursuits of me, myself, and I. I really want to help others, but unless I'm sure "I have enough," then my selfish inclination is to withhold from sacrificially making a difference in the lives of other people. The truth is that we aren't even capable of being selfish very well. Yesterday's self spent so much that today's self clings to whatever is left, neglecting tomorrow's self. Only Jesus can deliver us from our relentlessly selfish pursuits. It's not until the Lord is in charge as our shepherd that we shall not want. Until Jesus fills this void, we are left wanting something we cannot achieve and chasing shadows of things that do not exist.

WHEN WE CONFUSE OUR SIGNIFICANCE WITH OUR PROMINENCE, WE STRIVE TO VALIDATE OURSELVES THROUGH BEWILDERING PURSUITS.

A businessman went to Mexico for vacation. One day, he noticed a local bringing in his catch for the day. He struck up a conversation about fishing and how he could turn this into a leveraged source of income as an expanding fishing business. He explained that if he just stayed out a little longer, he could catch more fish to sell. The fisherman explained that he caught enough for his family by noon. The businessman asked what he did with the rest of his time, and the fisherman responded, "I sleep late, spend time with my family, and take siestas."

The businessman went into consultant mode explaining how he could help him turn this into a great source of income. He explained the progression of more time fishing produces an income that buys a bigger boat and eventually leading to owning several boats with several crews working hard to make more money. The fisherman asked what would happen after this. The businessman laughed, explaining he would become very wealthy like he had done and could visit small coastal villages sleeping late and spending time with his family.

Life-giving principles are discovered in the fact that greater satisfaction and blessing is associated with what we give rather than what we receive. This clarifies how the pursuit of getting more for me without giving into the lives of others leaves the trendy trinity dissatisfied, unfulfilled, and in want. There is evidence to suggest that you could become the richest person in the world and still be completely frustrated, straining to find purpose beyond everything this temporal world has to offer. One of the wealthiest and most powerful kings in the history of the world put pen to paper and clearly stated how success is completely incapable of satisfying our lives.

The author of Ecclesiastes was Solomon. As the king of a very prosperous and powerful nation, he had more wealth, power, and fame than you and I will ever, ever, ever, ever, ever…ever have. Solomon personally explored and experienced everything he desired, refusing himself no pleasure. There appears to be nothing Solomon could think of that he did not try yet concludes over and over in this curious writing that it was all "meaningless." Over the course of twelve chapters in the book of Ecclesiastes, he uses the Hebrew word that translates *meaningless* thirty-eight times.

A lack of purpose produces a pointless existence that can never be resolved in the life Ecclesiastes describes as a life "under the sun," using this phrase twenty-nine times. Solomon wasn't just some philosopher speculating about what the value of experiencing everything under the sun might be. In Ecclesiastes 2, Solomon lists an exhaustive list of all he pursued: pleasure, laughter, drinking, partying, building, planting, developing parks, gardens, reservoirs, groves of trees, herds, flocks, silver, gold, treasures, singers, and entertainers, and all kinds of women from all kinds of places.

After all these amazing experiences, many people would think this man would be fulfilled in every way. However, Solomon begins his writings with this not-so-chipper introduction:

> The words of the Teacher, son of David, king in Jerusalem: "Meaningless! Meaningless!" says the Teacher. "Utterly meaningless! Everything is mean-

ingless." What does man gain from all his labor at
which he toils under the sun? (Ecclesiastes 1:1–3, NIV)

Frustration, sarcasm, and cynicism abound in his empty
conclusions about this "life under the sun." These sarcastic
verses reveal the limitations of all human experience when
confined to the pursuit of the trendy trinity of me, myself,
and I. Life under the sun speaks of a life that is void of
heavenly purpose. This is when we stop living and merely
exist, resembling the existence of animals.

Animals seem very content to just be what they are. As
humans, created in the image of God, we have something in
us driving us to imagine more than what we are. Little boys
turn a plain stick into a mighty weapon, and when my
daughters were little, they could
imagine a majestic tea party of
magnificent proportion. We are
filled with a capacity to dream
beyond our existence! We are created to experience purposes
beyond our selfish pursuits.
"God…has planted eternity in
the human heart…" (Ecclesiastes
3:11, TLB).

Eternity planted in your heart
will require you to live a life

> ONLY GOD'S
> ETERNAL PURPOSES
> REVEALED IN THIS
> TEMPORAL LIFE
> MOVE US FROM
> MERELY EXISTING
> TO TRULY LIVING.

beyond your life in order to be fulfilled. True legacy is not determined by what you leave when you die but by what you give while you live. We must learn to be generous to others consistently.

We want to live well, but our foremost efforts should be to help others live well (1 Corinthians 10:24, MSG). To be a Christian is to be part of the universal body of Christ, just as being born is to be part of universal humanity. In the same way, it is God's plan for every human being to be born into a family to identify with that family; it is also God's plan for every believer to identify with a congregational family. God brings us together in congregational families to serve his purposes and to leave our world a better place! It is important that we work together to serve His eternal purposes as our foremost priority and concern. For some reason, the eternal purposes of God don't seem to be steering the ship in many ways in the church of our generation.

As a lead pastor to our congregation and an external elder to several other ministries, I am privy to a lot of church drama. Some would give up on the idea of a congregational family because of the abundance of immaturity that exists in the church. Of course, family drama is abundant in our own homes, and giving up on our family only complicates and multiplies the drama. Giving up on family isn't the answer, but it certainly does seem that church should be about something more than immature pursuits and childish conflict. So much of what is taking place in the church today is the result of our self-absorbed lives.

It's more than just cliché to say we need Jesus to be delivered from selfish behaviors. Clearly Jesus came to empower us to shift our focus from the trendy trinity to the true Trinity. Mary

> AS THE CHURCH
> BICKERS OVER
> PETTY ISSUES,
> THE LOST
> DESPERATELY
> NEED JESUS.

and Martha had a wonderful opportunity to host Jesus in their home. Mary was sitting at Jesus's feet in a posture of worship and adoration, while Martha was working and complaining about it.

Martha was distracted by all the preparations that had to be made. She came to him and asked,

> Lord, don't you care that my sister has left me to do the work by myself? Tell her to help me! "Martha, Martha," the Lord answered, "you are worried and upset about many things, but few things are needed—or indeed only one. Mary has chosen what is better, and it will not be taken away from her." (Luke 10:40–42, NIV)

> **WHEN WE ARE DISTRACTED FROM WORSHIP, WE ARE PRONE TO COMPLAIN.**

We don't have a whining problem. We have a worship problem. When we place our focus and attention on the love and the life of Jesus, we lose sight of the complaints that so easily hold our lives hostage. When we do experience a concern, we have a choice to make. We must choose to make a loving difference rather than merely making a critical point. If we use our voice for complaining more than praying about whatever is concerning us, we are selfishly misappropriating the God-given resource of our voice.

The buzzard and the hummingbird both fly over the desert. The buzzard searches out decaying carcasses lying in the open and feeds on them, while the hummingbird looks for sweet nectar of the beautiful wildflowers. Both find what they are looking for in the same desert. All of us tend to find what we look for. This is why two people can have two totally different experiences within the same context of that experience—whether it is church, family, work, etc.

A servant and a critic see the same problem but respond differently. God looked at darkness, and rather than complaining about the darkness or cooperating with it, he proclaimed light and transformed the situation! All of us and each of us must follow His example, having an empowering and encouraging faith to release transforming power to a fallen world. Anything less renders us as ineffective and unproductive Christians.

Discussion Questions

1. Why is it so easy to fall into the "me, myself, and I" trap? Name one person you trust to tell you the truth even if it hurts and explain why you would trust them to do so.

2. Search your heart about how you love, serve, and give in regard to both time and money. Do you love, serve, and give sacrificially, or is it more so an expression of convenience?

3. How would you describe the difference between dreaming big for God vs. embracing the very dreams of God?

4. When adversity comes, what does it take to move from complaining to worshiping? How are you at making this jump, and what can you do over this next week to make some kind of progress in this area of your life?

5. What about your perspective that would cause those closest to you to see more of a hummingbird perspective over the buzzard in your life?

Scripture References for Further Reading and Study

Ecclesiastes 1:1–3 (NIV)
Ecclesiastes 2
Ecclesiastes 3:11 (TLB)
1 Corinthians 10:24 (MSG)
Luke 10:40–42 (NIV)

Chapter 11

Don't Sell Your Birthright to the Clergy

IT WAS A Sunday morning, and I'd just finished preaching for three services. As I walked out to the lobby, there she was with a terrible look on her face that could have qualified as an artwork of disappointment. It was a masterpiece purposed to shame its intended viewer. "How are you?" I asked, feeling I had no other option than to take the bait. The response was forceful. The emotions were high. The conversation was charged with accusation, frustration, and a demand for change. "Pastor, I finally got my friend to attend church, and she needed prayer! She left right after the service ended, and our church never even prayed for her." My response stunned her. "That's terrible! Why didn't you pray for her before she left?" We are the church! We must be the church! Waiting for a pastor or a program to meet a need is to neglect our blessing and forfeit our birthright.

Abraham had been chosen by God to produce the lineage of the Messiah who would rescue the world. The riches of both heaven and earth had been entrusted to his care. Abraham's grandson, Esau, was born into this incredible legacy as a firstborn son. The firstborn received four benefits and responsibilities for the role of leading God's people: a special blessing, the office of high priest to his tribe, a position of leadership and authority, and procreative power. This special inheritance reserved for the firstborn could be forfeited by failing to develop and demonstrate commitment and service to God that are characteristic of priestly service and leadership in battle.

Genesis 25 explains the story where Esau's physical appetite took priority over his birthright. A conversation took place expressing desire, offer, consideration, and exchange. Even in our modern era, there is a valid, nonvoidable oral contract, which is enforceable in a court of law under certain circumstances. Esau did not value his birthright. He was a man driven by his appetite that was independent and would rather depend on his skill as a hunter rather than depend humbly on God to supply his needs. Esau was one of several examples we find in scripture who lost this valuable place in the legacy of God emerging in the history of humanity.

Ishmael lost his birthright to Isaac. Esau lost his birthright to Jacob. Reuben lost his birthright to Joseph. Manasseh lost his birthright to Ephraim. When the first-born sons lost their birthright, this special inheritance passed on to another son considered worthy of assuming that leadership role and procreative power. As I began exploring this in scripture, I discovered it was more common than I had realized. This not only occurred individually, but it also occurred congregationally.

> Then Moses went up to God, and the LORD... said..."tell the people of Israel...if you obey me fully and keep my covenant, then out of all nations you will be my treasured possession. Although the whole earth is mine, you will be for me a kingdom of priests and a holy nation. These are the words you are to speak to the Israelites." (Exodus 19:3–6, NIV)

> So Moses...set before them all the words the LORD had commanded him to speak. The people all responded together, "We will do everything the LORD has said." So Moses brought their answer back to the LORD. (Exodus 19:7–8, NIV)

God extended an invitation for these people who had just been liberated from slavery to become a royal priesthood, a holy nation, a people for God's own possession to proclaim His excellence in the earth. Their response was enthusiastic as they all responded together with an excitement for all the benefits this would provide for them. When Moses returned to the mountain with the acceptance of the people, it would appear that God also responded with enthusiasm.

> Mount Sinai was covered with smoke, because the LORD descended on it in fire. The smoke billowed up from it like smoke from a furnace, and the whole mountain trembled violently. As the sound of the trumpet grew louder and louder, Moses spoke and the voice of God answered him. (Exodus 19:18–19, NIV)

What happened next is one of the saddest portions of scripture ever written. The entire congregation of people abandoned their birthright as they deferred to Pastor Moses, asking him to go and meet with God on their behalf. Their appetite for comfort exceeded their desire to answer God's call. In a very real way, they sold their birthright to their ministry leader.

> When the people saw the thunder and lightning and heard the trumpet and saw the mountain in smoke, they trembled with fear. They stayed at a

distance and said to Moses, "Speak to us yourself and we will listen. But do not have God speak to us or we will die." Moses said to the people, "Do not be afraid. God has come to test you, so that the fear of God will be with you to keep you from sinning." The people remained at a distance, while Moses approached the thick darkness where God was. (Exodus 20:18–21, NIV)

The Israelite congregation was willing to give offerings and gather to listen to Moses after he would go and meet with God. Moses would fast, pray, be enriched in God's presence, and minister to people in the way God had desired for the entire congregation to experience. This story of the birthright exchange is still happening today. Jesus came extending an invitation that resembles the invitation from God found in Exodus.

> But you are a chosen race, a royal priesthood, a holy nation, a people for [God's] own possession, that you may proclaim the excellencies of Him who has called you out of darkness into His marvelous light. (1 Peter 2:9, NAS)

We don't mind being Christians gathering as the church to listen to sermons. We are even willing to give, especially if the sermons are inspiring and the ministry is engaging. The problem is that most of us are more committed to our comfort than we are devoted to our call. We are called to fast, to pray, to be enriched by God's presence and minister to people in a way that resembles the sacrificial example of Jesus Christ. It is more convenient to rely on the pastoral ministry of our leaders than to provide personal ministry to others and become fruitful. Jesus clearly taught that true disciples produce fruit and not just a little bit, but in his words, "much fruit."

> I am the vine; you are the branches. If you remain in me and I in you, you will bear much fruit; apart from me you can do nothing. If you do not remain in me, you are like a branch that is thrown away and withers; such branches are picked up, thrown into the fire and burned. If you remain in me and my words remain in you, ask whatever you wish, and it will be done for you. This is to my Father's glory, that you bear much fruit, showing yourselves to be my disciples. (John 15:5–8, NIV)

Tracy decided we needed to have a garden. Six tomato plants produced a surprising quantity of tomatoes. Before we knew it, we had extra bags of tomatoes sitting by the front door just in case somebody were to come by. Anybody who came to our door left with tomatoes. We learned that we had to establish a strong rhythm of giving these tomatoes away, or they would start attracting little bugs that came to devour. When you become fruitful, you will soon realize that the fruit of your life is not just for you. God gives fruitfulness so others can be fed from the abundance of your life. When you become fruitful, you must give into the lives of others. Or the very thing God intended to bless you with begins attracting devourers with destructive effects.

> **WHAT CONCERNS YOU IS A CLUE TO YOUR CALL.**

A God-given concern can drive you to fruitful ministry if you allow your concern to produce compassion. A God-given concern that does not produce fruitfulness in your life will begin to attract devourers. Concerns make way for compassion when we do something about them. Concerns make way for complaints when we expect somebody else to do something about them.

A family had attended our church for a few years. We had been very involved in helping them on many levels as they were truly a family in need. One Sunday, they arrived at church to discover that we had purchased a really nice car to present to them that morning. The car was full of gasoline, and it was also full of groceries to help with their overall budget. They loved their pastor, and they loved their church family! Interestingly, within just one year, this same family came in to let me know they were leaving the church, and their explanation astonished me. They explained they were leaving because our church didn't really carry a burden for families in need.

In honesty, I had a lot of things I could have said, knowing they were going to drive the car we gave them to their new church every week. Instead, I tried to learn from this conversation. Finally it emerged as they described having such a heart for homeless people and families who are struggling in such severe ways. Their frustration was that our church wasn't doing enough to reach out and help these people. I encouraged them to consider the cross that God had fashioned for their shoulder as they would go to another church. Rather than looking for a church that is doing what we want to see the church doing, perhaps we need to do what we are burdened to do, so we are helping our church become more effective at fulfilling God's call.

The enemy tries to take the very call God gave us to awaken others and use that to motivate us to judge them for not carrying our burden. A God-given concern drives us to effective ministry when submitted to the Lord and actively expressed with love. God's wisdom is a collective counsel that's discovered by validating the parts that each of us carry. As soon as we divide ourselves from others because they don't have our same passion or concern, we've lessened God's wisdom in our lives.

If we choose not to be constructive with our concern, it easily becomes a complaint producing toxic attitudes, and ultimately a septic life poisoning the lives of those around us. The enemy's plan is to convert concerns into complaints to sift us, and as many as he can with us, into an unhealthy frustration with the church! The temptation is to have a burden, tell a pastor, and wait to see if the church really cares. When we make institutional demands because of our individual burdens, we are taking a cross God designed to fit our shoulder and attempting to transfer that burden to someone else. When this happens, our God-given passion becomes a judgmental weapon the enemy uses to produce division. God's way of getting everything done is to give everybody a different burden. Our response to that burden will either produce life or it will produce death.

Chester Howard was a godly man who loved Jesus, a loving husband and a wonderful father. He was absolutely unbeatable in checkers, and even to his final days, I had given it my best effort. One day after Mr. Howard was well into his eighties, he had a serious heart issue. The doctors were astonished to find out how little blood was getting through his heart. One of the main arteries was completely blocked. This would be impossible except somehow his heart had made provision, passing blood flow through veins that created a natural bypass—a very rare occurrence. The heart didn't ask the head for permission. The heart simply did what it needed to do to meet the need. To be effective, the church must become a community of loving, caring organic relationships that respond to the promptings of God and the needs of others.

WHEN CHURCH IS REDUCED TO PASTORS PRODUCING PROGRAMS, WE ARE ATTRACTING AN AUDIENCE RATHER THAN EMPOWERING AN ARMY.

God desires to awaken believers to the work He deposited like seeds as His assignment in our lives. There is something God wanted done that makes you necessary. You are not an accident or an experiment. You are a purposed assignment from God to your family, your city, and our world!

There were about fifty of us who went to Juarez, Mexico, on a mission trip. We practiced the language, discussed the customs, fasted, prayed, and prepared in every way. Over the course of five days, we reached out in the streets caring for others, praying for their needs, and expressing the love of Jesus in every way we could. Can you imagine what would happen to that city if five hundred people would become fluent in the language, become culturally aware of the customs, and relocate there? These people would be a mobilized army of God infiltrating, over time, into the educational system as teachers, the business structure as business leaders, and the governmental network as influential officials.

It's easy to consider how these five hundred people could turn this entire community upside down for Christ! How many people has God gathered to your church family? We are this group of missionaries who know the language, understand the culture, and have jobs in strategic areas of influence. The question is simply, will we embrace our call to a "missional" life?

Discussion Questions

1. What motivates a person to quickly respond to a need they see in their church family?
2. What causes a person to neglect or avoid responding? What do those who neglect being involved miss out in life and ministry?
3. Can you think of an area in your church family where you could respond this week to make it better or be involved to more effectively contribute to the overall vision of sharing Christ as a church family?

4. What are some specific things that concern you, and how can they translate more effectively into compassion rather than complaints?

5. Describe somebody you know who has effectively discovered their God-given assignment. What is it about their life that could inspire you to do the same for yours?

Scripture References for Further Reading and Study

Genesis 25
Exodus 19–20
1 Peter 2:9 (NAS)
John 15:5–8 (NIV)

Church is a Verb

IN THE THIRD century, the church began establishing its presence in cities all over the world in an amazing way. Huge cathedrals were being built in major cities throughout England and Europe. Massive structures were established to communicate the presence of the church in a very dominant way. As impressive as these structures are, the presence of buildings will never change society. Church is not about a place where we attend or a description of who we are. Church is about how we live and what we do as the expression of Christ and His Kingdom in the earth!

Jesus died to mobilize the church to be a verb—not an institutionalized religion! There are three types of verbs: action verbs, linking verbs, and helping verbs. In the same way, the church should be about acting, linking, and helping. We are not called to a place. We are called to a people. The true Gospel is all about God's desires at work in God's people in honest and authentic ways.

A man I met shared how he was flying into JFK Airport with two first-class upgrades in his pocket, which would grant him access into the VIP lounge. He had an extended layover before flying out of the country, and he'd planned to relax in the comfortable leather chairs and enjoy free food. The lady seated next to him on the flight inquired with the flight attendant about an old friend of hers she had seen in first-class on the plane hoping to sit with her. The attendant politely explained that she could not be moved up from coach. The Holy Spirit prompted the man to give one of his upgrades to her, costing him the lounge for his layover. After an internal argument with God, he obeyed and handed her one of the tickets telling her to give it to the attendant, and she would be able to sit with her friend.

There were two attendants flying standby who happened to be seated behind them on the flight. They heard the conversation and knew the value of these upgrades, making comments to each other about how generous it was. The lady beside him heard their discussion, and soon, the situation became a conversation. So finally, he offered an explanation. He told her that he didn't want to give her the upgrade, but the Lord asked him to do so and that Jesus is much nicer than he is. She had pressed the call button to request to be upgraded, but when the attendant came, she told her never mind because she wanted to stay in her seat. That day, he led her to Jesus on the flight.

This is, perhaps, the purest expression of the Gospel of Jesus Christ I've ever heard. Rather than presenting ourselves as Christians doing our best to be Christlike, we should simply die to ourselves and let Jesus live through us! John 8 reveals that Jesus is the light of the world. Matthew 5 reveals that we are the light of the world. When we listen to his desires and respond to his prompting to care for others, His Light is revealed through our surrendered, available lives. It is this rich deposit of Christ within us that must emerge and be revealed to our world if the lost are to be attracted to the goodness of God.

Weekly we gather approximately two hundred high school students into our small auditorium for school chapel. Over the years, I've stood before this gathering of students on many occasions. One time I stood there speaking, a rather unruly student decided he needed to have a conversation with his friend. Initially, I alluded to the issue, mentioning how I'd appreciate it if everybody would please pay attention. Ultimately, after the more subtle approach wasn't working, I had the young man stand up and go to the principal's office. I was direct, and I felt totally justified. Afterward I went to the office to meet with him and with our principal, and we had a very firm conversation. The young man was humiliated that day having been singled out in front of all of his peers. And my opinion was that it served him right!

That night, I went home to my family. We had a nice dinner and a peaceful evening together. When Tracy and I went to bed, I remember taking her by the hand thanking God for a great day. As I rolled over to go to sleep, I felt the Holy Spirit was saying to me that the young man I humiliated didn't have a great day. My mind then began to wander as I pondered what he might be feeling at that very moment in time. Suddenly, I went from feeling justified to feeling convicted that I had been too hard on him. I prayed for him as I went to sleep.

The next morning, I made my way to this young man's class. As I walked in, the teacher gave me the floor, and I acted very arrogant on purpose to make the point more effectively. "Who is the man at this school which is a ministry of our church?" I asked. The class was quiet as I noticed a parent who was there to observe that day, making this a little more complicated. Finally a student near the back said, "You are, Pastor Lawrence." My disposition completely changed at that moment as I explained, "No, I'm not the man. Jesus is the man, and he had a conversation with me last night about how unhappy he was with the way I treated this young man yesterday in chapel." I explained the entire story and openly apologized to this student, asking him to forgive me that day. It's possible that my discussion that day was more impacting than all the sermons I'd preached in that school over the years combined.

It is all too easy to justify self-absorbed attitudes and perspectives. God's purposes are progressively revealed and gradually released as we become increasingly faithful with the seasons and stages at hand.

If you are faithful in little things, you will be faithful in large ones. But if you are dishonest in little things, you won't be honest with greater responsibilities (Luke 16:10, NLT). Discovering humility on today's level positions us to embrace God's strength and power on the next level God has already prepared for us. Conquering our pride on new levels and discovering a greater revelation of humility seems to be a prerequisite to promotion in God's kingdom. No good father gives a child more than they can handle too early. Sometimes God is preparing the place for us, but sometimes God is preparing us for the place. This is why we shouldn't be surprised if it takes about twenty years to become an overnight success. Breakthrough into a new level is not a place to arrive and relax. When we break into new levels, we are picking a fight on a brand new level. Previous faith for new levels will stress us out. Previous humility for new levels leaves us ill-equipped,

> WHEN WE ARE DISTRACTED BY SELFISH MOTIVES, WE BECOME HIJACKED FROM THE PURPOSES OF GOD.

untrained, and unqualified for dangerous battles, conflicts, and confrontations.

"Godless rulers throw their weight around, how quickly a little power goes to their heads…" (Matthew 20:27, MSG). Power must be handled carefully and correctly! My daughter just got her driver's permit, and it has been unnerving to see a fifteen-year-old behind the wheel of a three-thousand-pound vehicle traveling seventy miles per hour down a highway, swerving in and out of traffic with semitrucks all around at times. There have been a few times I have had to intervene. A teenager can easily get into trouble because they simply cannot ever be fully prepared for this kind of power that is under their control. This is why I'm an advocate that the legal driving age should be more like mid to late-twenties. Okay, just a nervous dad talking. But the reality does exist that maturity is required to effectively handle power.

My daughter will never be allowed to take our car anywhere by herself if she doesn't first let me sit in the front seat, inspecting every move she makes, screaming for her to look out. She feels completely under the microscope, and rightfully so. She feels completely overcoached, and though this is probably true, there is also a great deal more coaching that she needs than she realizes. Everybody's feet reached the pedals before we were ready to drive. Everybody's body possessed the ability to reproduce before we were ready to parent children. It's just normal to feel like we're ready long before we are ready in almost every area of life.

The real question when it comes to handling power is this: are we able to carry the mantle of a leader while continuing to be a servant? St. Augustine rightfully said, "Pride changes angels into devils."[1] Margaret Thatcher said, "Being powerful is like being a lady. If you have to tell people you are, you aren't."[2] We find Jesus addressing these issues in Matthew 5 just before he begins to teach on being powerful and influential as salt and light. Just prior to this teaching, we find the renowned Beatitudes. Where does Jesus begin when he's preparing his disciples to handle being endowed by power from God's kingdom in the earth?

"Blessed are the poor in spirit, for theirs is the kingdom of heaven" (Matthew 5:3, NIV). Jesus had just come out of the wilderness launching into powerful ministry influence. Not only was he now considered powerful and influential by many; he was leading a group of men who would soon become very powerful and influential to their world.

Jesus prioritized this foundational teaching on being poor in spirit specifically and strategically prior to the

---

[1]   *Topical Encyclopedia of Living Quotations*, ed. Sherwood Wirt (Minneapolis: Bethany House Publishers, 1982), 115.

[2]   "Margaret Hilda Thatcher Quotes," retrieved March 20, 2016, http://www.quotes.net/quote/17983.

release of supernatural gifts carrying amazing potential. When we think of being powerful or influential, we normally don't think of being poor. Jesus is always bringing a heavenly perspective to our earthly way of thinking to help us see more from God's point of view. To embrace being poor in spirit is to identify how dependent we are on God, understanding that we are spiritually bankrupt without Him. We are absolutely powerless alone. Twelve-step programs always start at this point. Until we admit where we are and that we have no power over our situation alone, we can't build correctly with a true dependency upon God's power.

WE TEND TO WORK AT BEING STRONG AND SELF-SUFFICIENT, BUT GOD'S POWER SHOWS UP BEST IN WEAK PEOPLE. IN WEAKNESS, WE ARE MADE STRONG!

Blessed are those who disconnect from self-serving ambition and pride. As we humble ourselves before the Lord, we more readily humble ourselves before others, recognizing how desperately we all need him. A pastor was visiting with me one day, talking about how he'd grown up in church and didn't really have a past like mine. He referenced how passionate people who had such a past seem to be in his experience. It appears that it's easier for those who have been more openly sinful to be more indebted to God's grace. However, we can draw some erroneous conclusions here if we're not careful.

> Two men owed money to a certain moneylender. One owed him five hundred denarii, and the other fifty. Neither of them had the money to pay him back, so he canceled the debts of both. Now which of them will love him more? Simon replied, "I suppose the one who had the bigger debt canceled." "You have judged correctly," Jesus said. (Luke 7:41–43, NIV)

It would almost appear that Jesus is substantiating the idea that the more sinful a person was before receiving Christ, the more that person is capable of loving God. However, a closer look at scripture reveals that there is more to it than that: "For whoever keeps the whole law and yet stumbles in one point, he has become guilty of all" (James 2:10, NAS).

Notice every person who ever offends just one point of the law is guilty of all. Better behavior didn't make you any less guilty before you met Jesus. Everyone was completely sinful before Jesus and becomes completely righteous after knowing Him (2 Corinthians 5:21). The blessing of loving him more results from understanding just how "poor in spirit" we were. It's submission to the reality of our completely sinful state that positions us to be released to a greater revelation of grace and righteousness through God's power.

Interestingly, when Jesus fed the multitude, he took the bread, he blessed the bread, he broke the bread, and then he gave the bread. We love it when Jesus takes us, blesses us, and gives us. However, before he can give us to his greatest purposes, we must first be broken. Religion tries to tell us that it is our faithfulness that positions us to be used by God. The Bible actually reveals that it's our brokenness that positions us to be used by God.

The Hebrew word *shabar* translates as *breaks* in Psalm 29:5. This word also translates as *birth* in Isaiah 37:3. This same word translates as *food* in Genesis 42:1. Our bodies have the capacity to break down food so it can be used for nourishment. When we are broken and choose to remain in the hands of God, something will be born, and others will be nourished and encouraged as a result. Faith and hope demand birth from brokenness.

Salvation came through Christ's broken body (1 Corinthians 11:24). God's attention comes to a broken heart (Psalm 51:17). Victorious light came from broken pitchers (Judges 7). Oil came from a broken box (Mark 14:3). Provision for the multitude came from broken bread (Matthew 14:10). There is no question about the seed possessing life, but it is only when it dies that it can produce life (John 12:24). Religion requires faithfulness. Jesus responds to brokenness. We must be willing to be broken on a new level before the next level of influence is entrusted to our care.

This idea of submission preceding the release of power and authority is not unusual. Job promotions are commonly coupled with further training and preparation that have resulted from having embraced a certain set of ideas and behaviors of the organization. Police officers don't wear a badge before submitting to extensive training and preparation. It is commonly understood that you must be a great learner before you can become a great leader. "No horse gets anywhere until he is harnessed. No steam or gas ever drives anything until it is confined. No Niagara is ever turned into light and power until it is tunneled. No life ever grows until it is focused, dedicated and disciplined."[3]

Discussion Questions

1. Church is a verb! Describe yourself in regard to ways you are currently acting (actively making a difference), linking the lives of people who can encourage each other, and helping others in need?

---

[3] Alan M. Bryan, *My God And Myself* (Smithfield: Success Dynamics), p. 43.

2. Pride is such a subtle enemy. What are some ways pride can show up undetected? How can we more effectively battle against this enemy?

3. What does it mean to you to be "poor in spirit"?

4. What is the difference between faithfulness and brokenness? How can we purpose every day to be more broken in the hands of our wonderful Savior so we can be more of an expression of his love to our world?

Scripture References for Further Reading and Study

Luke 16:10 (NLT)
Matthew 20:27 (MSG)
Matthew 5:3 (NIV)
Luke 7:41–43 (NIV)
James 2:10 (NAS)
2 Corinthians 5:21
1 Corinthians 11:24
Psalm 51:17
Judges 7
Mark 14:3
Matthew 14:10
John 12:24

Conclusion

Activate Your Destiny

NOBODY BUYS A treadmill thinking how great it will be to hang clothes on when they're one day trying to pick out the right outfit. However, many a treadmill have become neglected and reduced to the function of butlers with articles of clothing draped over them. Just because we have something doesn't mean we use it. Just because we have the mind of Christ doesn't mean we use the mind of Christ. Just because we have a destiny doesn't mean we have activated our destiny.

We must be passionately awakened to the purposes of God if we are to produce meaningful lives that are awakening God's

> DREAMS ARE NEVER BORN OUT OF INDIFFERENCE.

purposes in the lives of others. What has God purposed for you, and what will you do to begin to activate your destiny? Your life is precisely equipped with the exact experiences your dreams require. We must never let the deficiency of what we don't have distract us from the purpose of what we do have. The key to what is in your heart is always discovered in your hand.

God showed up to talk to Moses after forty years of feeling forgotten and worthless. His conversation was one of phenomenal magnitude requiring Moses to imagine something well beyond his existing capacity. God's total focus to get him where he needed to be is discovered in one single question: "What's that in your hand?" Everything that was being awakened in Moses's heart would be accessed by that which he held in his hand.

My prayer is that you have had something substantial awakened in your heart as you have read the chapters of this book. The key to anything awakened in your heart is discovered by what is in your hand. What relationship, skill, position, ability, or gift do you hold today that is part of God's plan to activate your destiny? It's all too easy to despise what's in our hand because it rarely resembles what's truly in our heart. If we do this, we sabotage what is in our hand and forfeit what is in our heart. What action can you take today, this week, or as immediately as possible, as a step forward in fulfilling what God has in store for your life? Your decisions determine your destiny, and your destiny awakens the destiny of others.

For years, the four-minute mile was considered not only unreachable, but many believed a successful attempt could result in the death of the runner potentially exceeding the physical limits of human endurance. Friday, May 7, 1954, Roger Bannister made history as he crossed the finish line with a time of 3 minutes and 59.4 seconds. No athlete in all the years of the Olympics or various competitions around the world had ever been able to run a mile in under four minutes. Within just weeks of Bannister's record-breaking run, several others accomplished this seemingly impossible accomplishment. It is as if the human race suddenly got faster in that summer of 1954.

More than one thousand people have broken the four-minute mile now. When someone breaks a barrier, the testimony of that success becomes convincing proof that others can achieve this accomplishment. The story God is writing about your life is a powerful tool to help others get past the limitations of their lives and discover amazing plans God will cause to emerge when we cooperate with his desires.

Before we were formed in the womb, God knew us. He planned for us and purposed our lives together for this generation. He made architectural deposits in our lives that are trying to emerge today. Recently, I heard a story of a reconstructive surgery that took place for a man whose nose was crushed in a terrible accident. A skillful doctor took a piece of ear cartilage and reconstructed it to look perfectly like the nose.

A few years later, there was a problem. The ear cartilage, now inside the nose, never forgot what it was always intended to be. The original design of the ear cartilage was trying to emerge inside the nose. Every few years, the surgeon would have to go back and operate again filing the ear cartilage down to keep the shape they want it to be. Despite this process of trying to keep the ear from emerging, the ear cartilage was never discouraged. Even before the grinding was over, it would continue its relentless ambition to return to its original design.

There is something inside every one of us trying to get back to its original design. The deepest part of you will always remember what it was meant to be. We never stop trying to be no matter what others try to make us become. No matter how far off course we go, there's always something deep within us that never stops trying to make us into what God originally designed us to be. Something in every one of us says you can file me down and try to make me into something else, but something in me knows there's something more to my life. Something deep inside us all knows we have an eternal purpose to be awakened and a destiny to be activated when we embrace who God truly made us to be, beyond all the religious confusion that may exist in our day.

May we passionately pursue God's presence and God's power as we engage in a fight that expands God's kingdom!

WE ARE THE GIANT KILLERS OF OUR GENERATION!

Let's kill some giants! Let's move some mountains!